HISTORICAL DEFIANCE

Historical Defiance

AFGHANISTAN'S UNYIELDING RESISTANCE LEGACY

MACK RAFEAL

UNIEK ENTERPRISES

Contents

INDEX

INTRODUCTION

Afghanistan, a country that is totally surrounded by land and is located at the intersection of Central Asia and South Asia, has a history that is marked by defiance and struggle. Because of its mountainous terrain, numerous ethnicities, and geopolitical significance, it has served as a battleground for opposing forces over the course of several centuries. The Afghan people, who are known for their stubborn character, have been subjected to a number of invasions and occupations; nonetheless, they have persistently fought external forces, thereby maintaining their independence and identity. The purpose of this essay is to investigate Afghanistan's historical defiance by analyzing significant instances that have contributed to the country's heritage of resistance and the enduring spirit that has characterized the Afghan people at all times.

The Great Game and the Imperialism of the British

During the 19th century, the British Empire and the Russian Empire engaged in a geopolitical war for power and influence in Central Asia. This conflict was known as the "Great Game," and it happened during the 19th century. Due to the fact that both empires were attempting to cement their supremacy in the region, Afghanistan became a focal point in this dynamic power play. Among the many examples of Afghanistan's endurance in the face of foreign intrusion, the First Anglo-Afghan War (1839-1842) stands out as a particularly noteworthy example.

In an effort to ensure the safety of their Indian empire, the British invaded Afghanistan and installed a puppet government there. When the British were confronted with a powerful opposition from Afghan tribal troops, they found themselves in the middle of a struggle that lasted for a long time and was often violent. Because of their expertise in guerilla warfare and their intimate familiarity with the difficult terrain of Afghanistan, the Afghans were able to successfully fight a resistance effort. In the end, the British were compelled to withdraw, which resulted in Afghanistan's independence being preserved but with the scars of the struggle still visible.

The Mujahideen and the Soviet Occupation of Afghanistan

When the Soviet Union invaded Afghanistan in 1979, it was the beginning of yet another negative chapter in the history of the country. The Soviet Union had the intention of supporting a communist government in Kabul; however, they were met with ferocious opposition by a variety of Afghan resistance groups who were generally referred to as the Mujahideen. The Afghan people, who were highly traditional and suspicious of foreign intrusion, banded together to oppose the invasion of the Soviet army.

The United States of America, Saudi Arabia, and other Western allies that saw the fight as a proxy war against the spread of communism provided backing to the Mujahideen, which consisted of a variety of factions with a wide range of ideologies. Afghanistan turned into a battlefield, and it was there that the unconquerable will of the Afghan people was once again put on display. Combined with the severe winters in Afghanistan and the dogged determination of the local fighters, the Mujahideen were able to wear down the superior Soviet military. This was accomplished through the efficient employment of guerilla tactics. The withdrawal of Soviet forces from Afghanistan in 1989 was a momentous occasion that marked a historic triumph for Afghanistan and was a crucial factor that contributed to the eventual downfall of the Soviet Union.

The Rule of the Taliban and the Post-Soviet Interval

Following the withdrawal of Soviet forces, Afghanistan entered a period of civil war, during which several Mujahideen factions competed with one another for control of the country. In the midst of the anarchy, the Taliban emerged as a formidable force, seizing control of Kabul in 1996 and implementing a stringent interpretation of Islamic law. Despite the fact that the Taliban's administration was characterized by cruelty and isolationism, it was also met with opposition from both within the country and from the international community.

Even though they were subjected to brutal conditions, the Afghan people were able to maintain aspects of their cultural identity and endure the rule of the Taliban with extraordinary endurance. The Taliban's treatment of women, restrictions on education, and destruction of cultural heritage sites were faced with opposition from inside the Taliban's own ranks. In the meantime, the world community, led by the United States, denounced the Taliban for their backing of international terrorists, which ultimately led to the invasion of Afghanistan in the year 2001.

The War on Terror and the Resistance of the Present Day

Al-Qaeda, the terrorist organization that was responsible for the assaults on the World Trade Center and the Pentagon, was being dismantled as part of the post-9/11 invasion that was carried out by the United States of America and its NATO allies with the intention of removing the Taliban regime from power. The struggle that ensued was drawn out and complicated, and it was this conflict that gave Afghanistan a new perspective on its history of resistance.

A tenacious insurgency emerged in the years that followed the original invasion, which resulted in the Taliban administration being overthrown in a short amount of time. After rearranging themselves, the Taliban began a fierce guerilla campaign against the soldiers from neighboring countries. The Afghan people, who were caught in the crossfire, showed an incredible amount of resilience in the face of the violence and instability that they were experiencing. In addition, the battle resulted in the formation of new resistance groups, each of which had its own set of complaints and reasons for fighting.

The country of Afghanistan continued to be steeped in violence despite the efforts that were made to construct a democratic and stable Afghanistan. As they navigated through shifting alliances, tribal loyalties, and external influences, the Afghan people demonstrated their resilience and their capacity to adjust to changing circumstances. This became clear as they maneuvered through these challenges. After the United States and NATO soldiers withdrew from Afghanistan in 2021, a significant turning point occurred, and Afghanistan was once again left to decide its own fate.

The Preservation of Heritage and the Resilience of Culture

The defiance of Afghanistan extends beyond its armed resistance and encompasses the country's cultural resilience. There is a wealthy tapestry of art, literature, and customs that have endured the test of time that can be found inside the nation. Afghan artisans and scholars have persisted to make works that honor the heritage of the country, despite the hurdles that have been posed by invasions and strife.

Before the Taliban destroyed them in 2001, the Buddhas of Bamiyan, which were ancient monuments carved into the cliffs of central Afghanistan, were considered to be emblematic symbols of the cultural wealth of the nation. This act of cultural vandalism was criticized by the international community, and attempts to protect and restore Afghanistan's cultural heritage gained pace as a result. Individuals and organizations put forth a lot of effort to document, safeguard, and restore historical sites, manuscripts, and artifacts. They did this because they understood the need of cultural preservation in the face of external dangers.

The Prospects for Afghanistan's Resistance Movement in the Future

In spite of the fact that Afghanistan is about to enter a new phase of its history, which will be characterized by the withdrawal of foreign forces and the return of Taliban authority, the legacy of historical defiance continues to be deeply imprinted in the psychology of the country. The people of Afghanistan, who have been subjected to centuries of conflict and occupation, continue to fight for their right to self-determination and to oppose meddling from outside sources.

The international community is an essential component in the process of determining the future of Afghanistan. There is potential for the reconstruction of Afghanistan and the empowerment of its people to be aided by humanitarian initiatives, diplomatic engagement, and assistance for civil society. It is vital to prioritize inclusive government, human rights, and sustainable development in order to secure a more stable and prosperous future for Afghanistan. This can be accomplished by learning from the mistakes that have befallen Afghanistan in the past.

A tribute to the resilient spirit of the Afghan people in the face of hardship is the historical defiance that Afghanistan has displayed throughout its history. Afghanistan's resistance heritage has influenced its history and defined its character from the days of the Great Game to the current withdrawal of foreign forces. This legacy has been passed down from generation to generation. The Afghan people have demonstrated a remarkable resilience that transcends geopolitical concerns, as evidenced by their capacity to survive invasions, adapt to changing conditions, and preserve their cultural legacy.

In order for Afghanistan to successfully traverse the challenges of its post-withdrawal age, the international world must acknowledge the significance of providing assistance to the Afghan people for the reconstruction of their homeland. For the purpose of cultivating a future that is worthy of the ambitions of Afghanistan's resilient population, it is essential to recognize and respect the historical resistance that Afghanistan has displayed. It is only through cooperation, empathy, and a profound comprehension of Afghanistan's complicated past that the international community will be able to make a contribution to a tomorrow that is more secure and prosperous for this tenacious nation.

1. **Afghanistan's historical significance**

   Afghanistan is a country that is located at the intersection of Central Asia and South Asia, and it has a history that is just as complex and varied as its rocky geography. As a result of its advantageous location, it has served as a significant hub for the exchanges between various civilizations and empires throughout the course of history. Afghanistan's historical significance is woven into the fabric of human civilization, from the ancient Silk Road to the modern geopolitical stage. It is characterized by cultural exchange, conflict, and a resilient spirit that has survived for centuries. Afghanistan's history is intertwined into the fabric of human civilization.

   Places of Geographical Confluence

   It is because of Afghanistan's location that it has been given a special and vital role in the process of determining the path that history will take. Afghanistan is located at the intersection of a number of different cultures and civilizations. It is surrounded by Iran to the west, Pakistan to the east and south, Turkmenistan, Uzbekistan, and Tajikistan to the north, and China to the northeast. This confluence of influences has left an unmistakable impact on the identity of the country, transforming it into a cultural melting pot that is formed by the traditions of the Middle East, Central Asia, India, and Persian culture. Within the borders of Afghanistan, the old Silk Road, which was a network of trade routes between the East and the West, passed through the country. Places such as Heart and Balkh developed into important commercial and cultural exchange hubs during this time period. Not only did the Silk Road make it easier to trade products, but it also served as a channel through which ideas, faiths, and philosophical perspectives could find their way to people.

This historical trading route transformed Afghanistan into a cultural cross-roads, where the currents of Buddhism, Zoroastrianism, Hinduism, and subsequently Islam converged and coexisted. Eventually, Islam became the dominant religion in Afghanistan.

The Historical Tapestry: Empires and Successive Conquests

The rise and collapse of empires that attempted to control Afghanistan's crucial terrain is a significant part of our understanding of the country's historical significance. Alexander the Great embarked on a campaign through the Persian Empire, which ultimately led him to the gates of what is now Afghanistan. The region has been a witness to the conquests that Alexander the Great performed. The mingling of Greek and Persian civilizations during this time period left an indelible mark on the region's art, architecture, and language. This heritage will forever be remembered.

After a number of centuries had passed, the Islamic conquests that took place in the seventh century wrote a new chapter in the history of Afghanistan. It was in this region that towns such as Ghazni and Heart flourished as centers of study, art, and science, and the region eventually became an important center of Islamic civilization. The cultural heritage of Afghanistan became an essential component of the larger Islamic world, making a significant contribution to the growth of Islamic academia and the arts.

Afghanistan experienced a significant transformation as a result of the Mongol invasions that took place in the 13th century and were commanded by Genghis Khan and his descendants. Cities were completely destroyed, inhabitants were uprooted, and the sociocultural landscape went through the process of undergoing enormous transformations. The indomitable spirit of Afghanistan, on the other hand, persisted, and during the 14th and 15th centuries, the province had a rebound under the Timurid Empire. This revival was characterized by a renaissance in art, literature, and architecture.

Colonial Intrigues, the Great Game of the World

Afghanistan's historical significance was given a new dimension in the 19th century when the "Great Game" between the British and Russian Empires began to take place. This game was played between Afghanistan and Russia. During this time period, the Russians were working to increase their influence southward, while the British were working to safeguard their Indian colonies. Because of its advantageous location, Afghanistan became a contentious territory for the colonial countries who were involved.

A number of wars that took place in Afghanistan throughout the 19th century, including the First Anglo-Afghan War (1839-1842) and following wars, demonstrated Afghanistan's resistance to foreign involvement.

The people of Afghanistan, who were strongly rooted in their tribal institutions, fought back vehemently against forces from the outside. As a result of the outcomes of these conflicts, Afghanistan gained a reputation for being the "Graveyard of Empires," a moniker that would continue to reverberate over the decades as other powers attempted to exert authority over its area.

Obsession by the Soviet Union and Resistance by the Mujahideen

Over the course of the latter half of the 20th century, Afghanistan was once again thrown into the spotlight of the international community, this time as the setting for the Soviet-Afghan War (1979-1989). In its efforts to support a communist administration in Kabul, the Soviet Union encountered resolute opposition from several factions of the Afghan Mujahideen. A protracted and ultimately successful guerrilla struggle was undertaken by the Afghan people, who were entrenched in a tradition of independence and were opposed to the occupation of foreign powers within their country.

It was a turning point in the geopolitics of the Cold War when the United States and its allies provided support to the Afghan resistance, which helped to strengthen the Afghan resistance. The triumph held by the Mujahideen not only brought an end to the supremacy of the Soviet Union in the region, but it also played a role in the eventual downfall of the Soviet Union itself. During this time period, the Afghan people demonstrated their will to protect their sovereignty in the face of enormous difficulties by demonstrating their high level of resilience.

Challenges Facing Modern Society: The War on Terror and Even Further

Afghanistan was confronted with significant challenges at the beginning of the 21st century, particularly in the wake of the attacks that occurred on September 11, 2001. In the year 2001, a coalition led by the United States of America invaded Afghanistan with the intention of completely removing Al-Qaeda and the Taliban administration from power. This event signaled the beginning of a new chapter in the history of Afghanistan, which would be defined by intricate geopolitics, insurgency, and efforts to construct a nation.

In the years that followed, Afghanistan was confronted with a variety of challenges, including those pertaining to governance, security, and economic development. In spite of the fact that they were once again caught in the middle of interventions from outside sources, the Afghan people have shown that they are resilient in the face of suffering. However, the path to stability proved to be elusive, as the nation continued to struggle with internal strife as well as pressures from the outside world.

Protecting the Heritage of Cultural Practices

In the midst of the difficulties brought on by the fighting, Afghanistan has also been confronted with the necessity of protecting its extensive cultural heritage. During the year 2001, the Taliban were responsible for the destruction of the Buddhas of Bamiyan, which brought the dangers that Afghanistan's historical sites face to the attention of the international community. The necessity of preserving the nation's identity and history was brought to light by the fact that efforts to document, protect, and repair cultural items gained pace.

It is clear that Afghanistan's cultural resilience is demonstrated by the fact that its traditional arts, crafts, and oral traditions have persisted over time. Not only does the preservation of cultural legacy serve as a demonstration of the tenacity of the Afghan people, but it also serves as a bridge that connects the past to the present, thereby developing a sense of continuity and identity.

The historical significance of Afghanistan is a complex story that spans multiple facets, including crossroads, conquests, and resiliency. Over the course of history, the nation has been at the intersection of numerous cultures and civilizations, from the ancient Silk Road to the contemporary geopolitical arena. Due to the fact that they have been fashioned by centuries of history, its people have consistently demonstrated an unconquerable spirit when confronted with challenges.

Taking into account Afghanistan's historical significance is absolutely necessary as the country works through the issues it is currently facing and looks to the future. In order to ensure that Afghanistan's rich history and cultural heritage continue to flourish, the international community plays a significant role in providing support for Afghanistan's attempts to reconstruct. The history of Afghanistan is one of perseverance, and it is through an understanding and appreciation of this history that a more secure and prosperous future may be formed for this amazing nation that is located in the center of Asia.

2. **Thesis statement: Unveiling Afghanistan's legacy of unyielding resistance**

Afghanistan, a country that is frequently referred to as the "Graveyard of Empires," has garnered a reputation for its unwavering spirit of resistance throughout the course of history. There is a tradition of persistent resistance that is firmly woven into the history of Afghanistan. This legacy can be seen in the rocky terrains that have witnessed the march of conquerors, as well as in the unique tapestry of cultures that constitute the identity of Afghanistan. Afghanistan has become a symbol of defiance against foreign forces, and this article will explore the historical, cultural, and geopolitical causes that have contributed to this transformation. The goal of this essay is to uncover the layers of this amazing legacy.

In the context of history, the cemetery of empires

"Graveyard of Empires" is a term that perfectly captures the historical role that Afghanistan has played as a strong hurdle to foreign powers who are striving to dominate the region. Throughout the course of history, the country has been a battleground for imperial ambitions due to its strategic location at the crossroads of Central Asia and South Asia. Afghanistan has been successful in thwarting attempts at external domination on multiple occasions, including those made by the Persians, Greeks, Mongols, and, more recently, the British and the Soviet parties.

The First Anglo-Afghan War, which took place in the 19th century, is a prime example of this resistance struggle. During the course of the British Empire's efforts to secure its Indian possessions, it encountered robust opposition from the Afghan people. The British soldiers were eventually forced to flee as a result of the hard terrain, as well as the determined Afghan rebels who employed guerilla tactics. Afghanistan's legacy as a nation that refuses to be tamed was established by this early occurrence, which left an everlasting impression on the country's history.

Obsession by the Soviet Union and Resistance by the Mujahideen

A significant turning point in Afghanistan's history of stubborn resistance is the Soviet-Afghan War, which took place from 1979 and 1989. When the Soviet Union attempted to support a communist administration in Kabul, it was met with violent hostility by several groups of the Afghan Mujahideen. The people of Afghanistan, who were firmly rooted in their tribal traditions and were hostile to the occupation by foreign forces, participated in a guerrilla war that lasted for a long time and finally was successful.

It is not simply a military accomplishment that the Mujahideen were successful in their resistance, but it is also a monument to the resiliency of the Afghan people. The fact that they were able to utilize the challenging terrain to their advantage demonstrated their capacity to adjust to the ever-shifting dynamics of combat. The assistance that Afghanistan got from the world community, particularly from the United States and its allies, highlighted the fact that the battle for independence in Afghanistan is recognized on a global scale. Afghanistan's heritage as a nation that could not be subjugated was reaffirmed by the Soviet withdrawal, which not only marked the end of a cruel battle but also reaffirmed Afghanistan's strength as a nation.

Control by the Taliban and Opposition from Within

There was a separate aspect of Afghanistan's resistance heritage that emerged during the time that the Taliban were in power in the latter part of the 20th century. In spite of the fact that the Taliban rule was attempting to enforce its rigorous interpretation of Islamic law, it encountered opposition and opposition from within the country. In spite of the fact that Afghan women, in particular, were subjected to the most severe consequences of the Taliban's harsh policies, they became images of silent defiance.

Despite the fact that the Taliban maintained an authoritarian government, there was a complicated web of opposition that thrived beneath the surface. Poetry and music were two examples of cultural manifestations that continued to exist underground. In order to educate themselves and their daughters in secret, women discovered several methods. The people of Afghanistan, although being dominated by forces from the outside, adhered to their identity and waited for an opportunity to restore their agency.

The War on Terror and the Challenges of the Present Times

Afghanistan faced a new set of obstacles in the years following the attacks of September 11, thanks to the invasion that was led by the United States and the ensuing efforts to build the nation. In spite of the fact that the primary objective was to bring down the Taliban administration and dismantle Al-Qaeda, the years that followed were marked by a persistent insurgency. Even though they were removed from power, the Taliban reorganized themselves and began a sustained fight against forces from other countries.

A tradition of uncompromising resistance continued to be passed down from generation to generation in Afghanistan as the Afghan people handled the challenges of a nation in change. The continuity of the historical narrative was proved by the ability to endure intrusions from the outside and to adjust to changing conditions. As a result of being caught in the crossfire of international ambitions, the Afghan people have once again become the builders of their own fate.

Internal Struggle and Pressures from the Outside World

Afghanistan went through internal instability in addition to the global problems it was experiencing. The path to stability in the nation was further complicated by the presence of factionalism and power conflicts among various political and ethnic groups among the population. Despite this, Afghanistan's history of resistance continued to exist. A future free from the shadows of war was something that the Afghan people yearned for. They were tired of warfare and intervention from foreign powers.

In 2021, the United States and NATO soldiers withdrew from Afghanistan, marking an important turning point in the country's previous history. As Afghanistan was once again confronted with the possibility of being ruled by the Taliban, concerns regarding the future of Afghanistan's tradition of relentless resistance began to surface. The people of Afghanistan, who had been through decades of conflict, found themselves at a crossroads where they faced both uncertainty and the optimism that tomorrow might be better.

The Maintenance of Cultural Identities

Not only does Afghanistan's resistance extend to the preservation of its cultural identity, but it also extends to the maintenance of violent battles. The demolition of the Buddhas of Bamiyan by the Taliban in 2001 garnered criticism from all across the world; nevertheless, it also brought to light the significance of cultural heritage as a symbol of resistance. In order to assert the nation's identity in the face of external threats, efforts were made to document, safeguard, and restore the rich cultural relics that Afghanistan possesses.

In the face of the chaos that is war, the Afghan people have demonstrated a remarkable level of resistance by resolutely committing themselves to the preservation of their cultural heritage. Even at the most difficult of times, the richness of Afghanistan's art, literature, and traditions serves as a source of strength due to the fact that it connects the past with the present and fosters a sense of continuity.

A multilayered narrative that transcends both time and situation, Afghanistan's legacy of unrelenting resistance presents a number of challenges. From the struggle against oppressive regimes to the invasions of empires, the Afghan people have consistently shown a spirit that refuses to be broken. This spirit has been displayed throughout the history of Afghanistan. The echoes of Afghanistan's past resistance continue to reverberate as a reminder of a nation that has endured, adapted, and persisted against all odds. This is happening at a time when Afghanistan is struggling with the issues it is currently facing and navigating an uncertain future. Not only does the revealing of Afghanistan's legacy of stubborn resistance disclose a history of struggle, but it also serves as a monument to the strength and tenacity that are ingrained in the very essence of this extraordinary nation.

Chapter 1

The Land and Its People

Afghanistan is a land that is characterized by its harsh terrain, numerous cultures, and a history that is engraved with resilience. It is located in the middle of Asia. With this essay, I will go on a complete examination of Afghanistan, diving into the delicate interplay between the country's terrain, the rich tapestry of its people, and the construction of a distinct national identity. The terrain of Afghanistan and the people who live there tell a story that extends beyond national boundaries and spans millennia. This story may be found in the towering peaks of the Hindu Kush as well as in the historic bazaars of Kabul.

A tapestry of mountains and valleys is what geography is all about

The regions that have shaped Afghanistan over the course of millions of years are reflected in the country's topography, which is a tribute to those influences. In addition to being dominated by the formidable Hindu Kush mountain range, the terrain of the country is a patchwork of rocky peaks, deep valleys, and dry plains for the most part. Not only does the Hindu Kush have peaks that achieve heights of more than 7,000 meters, but it also presents considerable hurdles to human habitation and communication. The Hindu Kush is a mountain range that is known for its breathtaking visual magnificence.

The geographical features of the nation have played a significant role throughout its history, affecting everything from the routes of trade to the military techniques that were employed. Because of the hilly landscape, Afghanistan has been referred to as the "Graveyard of Empires." This is because the steep terrain has functioned as a natural barrier. Armies that have invaded Afghanistan, beginning with the armies of Alexander the Great and continuing through Soviet forces in the 20th century, have struggled to overcome the obstacles that Afghanistan's rugged topography has presented.

Several rivers, including the Amu Darya and the Helmand, wind their way through the valleys, supplying significant amounts of water that are essential for agricultural production and the maintenance of populations. Agriculture, on the other hand, has historically been a difficult enterprise due to the limited availability of arable land, which has resulted in a dependence on trade and pastoral nomadism in a number of different places.

The Cultural Mosaic: Diversity in the Context of Unity

The cultural landscape of Afghanistan is a patchwork of many races, languages, and customs with each other. Pashtuns, Tajiks, Hazaras, Uzbeks, and other ethnic groups are among those that contribute to the complex tapestry that is Afghan society. The country is home to a multiplicity of ethnic groups. Every ethnic group contributes its own distinct language, traditions, and history, which results in a cultural environment that is rich in diversity.

The southern and eastern areas of Afghanistan are home to the Pashtun people, who make up the largest ethnic group in the country. In addition to being one of the official languages of the country, their language is known as Pashto. Dari, which is another official language, is spoken by the Tajik people, who are primarily located in the north of the country. Their cultural history is heavily affected by the traditions of the Persians. The Hazara people, who are known for their distinctive Mongol appearance, have a history that has been formed by a combination of Persian and Central Asian influences. They live in the central highlands.

The fact that Afghanistan is located at the intersection of Central Asia and South Asia is reflected in the country's diverse cultural landscape, which includes the languages that are spoken there. The official languages of Afghanistan are Dari and Pashto, both of which are members of the Indo-Iranian language family, which is connected to the Indo-European language family. A further factor that contributes to the linguistic diversity of the nation is the existence of a wide variety of regional languages and dialects.

Additionally, Afghanistan's cultural environment is characterized by a significant amount of religious variety. There are considerable Shia Muslim populations in Afghanistan, particularly among the Hazaras, despite the fact that the majority of Afghans adhere to the Sunni variant of Islam. Additionally, Sufi traditions, which are characterized by their mysticism and interpretations of Islam, have left an everlasting influence on the spirituality of Afghanistan.

Historical Footprints: Ancient Civilizations and Crossroads in International History

The history of Afghanistan is a tapestry that is woven with the historical footprints of ancient civilizations and the interactions of a variety of different cultures. Over the course of history, this area has served as a crossroads for a number of different empires and trade routes, which has contributed to the amalgamation of cultural aspects that characterize Afghanistan today.

In ancient times, the region that is today known as Afghanistan was a part of the Persian Empire. The Achaemenids and the Seleucids were the last rulers to rule over this region. An indelible mark was left on the region as a result of the conquests of Alexander the Great, which carried with them the influence of Hellenistic civilization.

The discovery of the city of Ai Khanoum in the northern region of Afghanistan serves as a testament to the cultural fusion that occurred during this time period between the cultures of Greece and Central Asia.

In Afghanistan, the Buddhist era was characterized by the construction of vast monastic complexes and the carving of the Buddhas of Bamiyan. This occurred mainly during the reign of the Kushan Empire. Despite the fact that they were tragically destroyed by the Taliban in 2001, these enormous statues were once emblems of Afghanistan's rich cultural heritage and its importance as a hub for Buddhist pilgrimage.

In the seventh century, the entrance of Islam marked the beginning of a new age, which had a significant impact on the cultural and architectural environment of Afghanistan. Because of their location at the intersection of the Islamic world, the Ghaznavid and Ghurid dynasties were instrumental in the propagation of Islamic civilization from one region to another. During the 14th and 15th centuries, the Timurid Empire, which had its capital in Herat, developed into a center of intellectual and cultural flowering.

Commerce and the Exchange of Cultures Along the Silk Road

Afghanistan was a crucial destination along the historic Silk Road due to its strategic placement at the crossroads of Central Asia and South Asia. Through the facilitation of the interchange of products, ideas, and civilizations between the East and the West, Afghanistan became a melting pot of influences. This network of trade routes was responsible for this transformation.

Numerous cities, including Heart and Balkh, flourished as thriving commercial and cultural hubs throughout this time period. The Silk Road was traveled by merchants from China, Persia, India, and other countries. These merchants brought with them silks, spices, and ideas that contributed to the cultural and intellectual development of Afghanistan. During this time period, the busy bazaars and caravanserais transformed into crucibles of creativity, serving as places where artisans and academics not only traded goods but also knowledge.

In addition, the Silk Road was a vital factor in the propagation of various human religions. The country of Afghanistan was a fruitful site for the development of Buddhism, Zoroastrianism, and eventually Islam, leaving behind a rich religious history. The Silk Road was responsible for facilitating centuries of encounters between people of different cultures, which resulted in the syncretic characteristic of Afghan culture, which is characterized by its capacity to take in and incorporate a wide range of influences.

Contemporary Obstacles: Struggle and the Capacity to Thrive

Afghanistan became a focal point of geopolitical confrontations throughout the latter half of the 20th century, which brought forth challenges that had never been seen before in the country's history. War between the Soviet Union and Afghanistan, which lasted from 1979 to 1989, was a terrible chapter in the history of the country. This war was distinguished by widespread destruction as a result of foreign interference and the subsequent development of the Taliban administration.

In spite of this, the Afghan people have demonstrated remarkable perseverance in the face of adversity. The Mujahideen, with the assistance of the international community, put up a fight against the Soviet forces, demonstrating their desire to protect their independence. On the other hand, during the succeeding period of Taliban administration, which was characterized by repressive policies and cultural limitations, there was an underground resistance that maintained the sense of Afghan nationality.

Following the events of September 11, 2001, a new phase of conflict emerged in Afghanistan as a result of the United States and its allies intervening in the country with the goal of removing the Taliban rule and eliminating terrorist networks. Despite being caught in the crosshairs of opposing interests, the Afghan people have once again shown that they are unwavering in their determination to persevere and rebuild.

Ensuring the Preservation of Heritage: Cultural fortitude

Afghanistan has endeavored to maintain its extensive cultural history, despite the difficulties that have been brought about by the fighting. The perseverance of the Afghan people in the face of external dangers is highlighted by the efforts that are being made to chronicle, safeguard, and restore historical places, manuscripts, and artifacts found in Afghanistan. Both organizations and people have exerted a great deal of effort in order to preserve the relics of long-lost civilizations and to guarantee that Afghanistan's cultural heritage would be preserved for future generations.

It is a proof of the commitment to preserve the heritage of the nation that the National Museum of Afghanistan was established in Kabul, despite the fact that it was faced with major hurdles when it was being established. A concerted effort to preserve Afghanistan's cultural assets is reflected in international cooperation for the restoration of historical sites. Some examples of these sites include the Citadel of Herat and the Minaret of Jam.

The history of Afghanistan is a story that spans millennia, and the land and people of Afghanistan are integral components of that story. A nation that exemplifies resilience and adaptation has been developed.

This nation has been shaped by its rough geography, numerous cultures, and rich history. Afghanistan is a country whose identity is intricately intertwined into the very fabric of its land and its people, from the ancient Silk Road to the present problems of conflict.

Considering that Afghanistan is currently at a crossroads in its future, struggling with the intricacies of nation-building and geopolitical dynamics, it is of the utmost importance to have a solid understanding of the interplay that exists between the country's geography, culture, and history. The unwavering determination of the Afghan people is demonstrated by the continued preservation of their legacy, which includes both tangible and intangible aspects of their culture. The land and its people, which are entwined in a complicated dance of continuity and change, provide a story of a nation that has endured the storms of time while still keeping its own identity within the variegated mosaic of human civilization.

1.1 Geographic features shaping Afghan character

A testament to the enormous influence that Afghanistan's geographical features have had on the country's character is the fact that Afghanistan's geography is both rough and diverse. Afghanistan's topography has not only established the country's physical boundaries, but it has also left an indelible stamp on the psyche of its people. From the towering peaks of the Hindu Kush to the parched expanses of its plains, Afghanistan's environment has left an indelible impact. In this essay, we investigate the ways in which the characteristics of the Afghan landscape have contributed to the development of the Afghan character, including the attributes of resiliency, adaptation, and a profound connection to the land.

The Unforgiving Terrain Constitutes a Natural Stronghold

Afghanistan is characterized by its rough and hilly landscape, which is dominated by the imposing Hindu Kush mountain range. This environment has been a significant contributor to the formation of the country's personality. The phrase "Graveyard of Empires" itself is a reflection of the historical perseverance of the Afghan people against foreign invasions. The difficult geology of Afghanistan serves as a natural fortification, and the phrase itself symbolizes this resilience.

With peaks that reach heights of more than 7,000 meters, the Hindu Kush mountain range provides a complex network of valleys and passes, which makes military operations a challenging endeavor. The rugged hilly terrain has been a challenge for invading forces throughout history, beginning with the armies of Alexander the Great and continuing through the Soviet Union in the 20th century. One of the factors that has contributed to Afghanistan's reputation as a region that is resistant to external control is the inherent difficulties of navigating such settings.

The character of Afghanistan, which was shaped in the fires of these towering peaks, exemplifies the spirit of defiance and independence. The steep terrain has not only served as a physical barrier, but it has also evolved into a symbol for the tenacity that is the defining characteristic of the Afghan identity today. The ability of the Afghan people to adapt to the difficulties presented by the mountains has instilled in them a sense of self-reliance as well as a profound connection to the territories through which they originated.

In the face of arid plains and limited water sources, agriculture faces a significant challenge

Plains and valleys are equally important components of Afghanistan's topography, despite the fact that the hilly terrain constitutes a considerable portion of the country's profile. The dry plains, in conjunction with the restricted water sources, present agriculture with a number of significant problems. Due to the limited availability of arable land, people have historically been forced to adopt a flexible approach to their means of subsistence, which has resulted in a dependence on commerce, pastoral nomadism, and innovative agricultural solutions.

The Afghan people have developed a sense of resourcefulness and pragmatism as a result of the difficulties they have encountered in the agricultural sector. Agriculture in Afghanistan is characterized by its adaptability, as evidenced by the use of terraced farming in hilly locations, the development of innovative irrigation systems, and the cultivation of resistant crops that are suitable to grow in arid circumstances. The ability to eke out sustenance from difficult settings has been ingrained in the spirit of the Afghan people, turning them into a people who are tenacious and resilient in the face of adversity.

Additionally, the shortage of water has contributed to the development of a culture of communal cooperation, which includes the utilization of common irrigation systems and methods for water management. It is a reflection of a profound appreciation of the connectivity that exists between the land and its inhabitants that this sense of community responsibility in the management of essential resources exists.

Crossroads of Cultures: The Impact of the Silk Road on the World History

The geographical location of Afghanistan, which is at the intersection of Central Asia and South Asia and is situated along the old Silk Road, has been a significant contributor to the formation of its personality. A steady stream of people, ideas, and goods passed through Afghanistan as a result of the Silk Road, which was a network of commercial routes between the East with the West. A spirit of openness and adaptation has been fostered as a result of this cultural interaction, which has left an indelible stamp on the identity of the Afghan people.

As a result of the contacts that took place along the Silk Road, Afghanistan became a melting pot of different cultures. City bazaars, such as those found in Herat and Balkh, evolved into bustling hubs of commercial activity and cultural collaboration. Traders, intellectuals, and craftspeople from a wide range of cultural and religious origins traveled over the Silk Road, bringing with them a broad array of languages, religious practices, and cultural standards.

This interaction between people of different cultures has had an effect on the Afghan character, which represents a sense of cosmopolitanism and an embrace of diversity. The ability to traverse between various cultural influences and incorporate them into the fabric of Afghan society has become a defining characteristic of the national character of Afghanistan. As a result of its long history as a cultural crossroads, Afghanistan has evolved a resilience that is a direct result of its acceptance of a wide variety of ideas and points of view.

The Construction of Communities in the Context of Tribalism and Geographic Isolation

The hard geographical aspects of Afghanistan, such as the steep terrain and the wide distances that separate villages, have played a role in the development of groups that are closely tied together and a social structure that is based on tribalism. Isolation brought forth by the mountains and valleys has resulted in the formation of various tribal identities, each of which has its own set of customs, traditions, and social systems.

In Afghanistan, tribalism is not only a social organization; rather, it is a way of life that is strongly embedded in the topography of the country. Throughout history, the mountains have served as natural boundaries, influencing the distribution of resources and determining the domains of many tribes. There is a sense of loyalty and mutual support among members of tribal communities because of the close-knit structure of these communities, which is bonded by shared histories and physical proximity.

This tribal system has had a significant impact on the Afghan character, which places a great focus on familial bonds, community cohesion, and a collective ethos. In times of external threats or hardships, the tribal affiliations have frequently provided a source of strength and resilience for the people. The geographical isolation of many communities has resulted in a need for intra-community networks for survival, which has contributed to the development of a strongly established sense of communal identity.

When it comes to urban centers and cultural hubs, striking a balance between modernity and tradition

On the other hand, the urban centers of Afghanistan have also played a key role in developing the national character, despite the fact that Afghanistan's geographical features have historically had an impact on rural life and tribal populations.

Kabul, Herat, and Kandahar are examples of cities that have served as cultural hubs. These cities are places where a variety of influences come together and contribute to the development of a contemporary identity for Afghanistan.

New dynamics have been brought into Afghan society as a result of urbanization, which has been fueled by a variety of causes including trade, education, and governance. The adaptability of the Afghan character is shown in the combination of modern influences and ancient traditions that may be found in metropolitan centers from Afghanistan. The dynamic culture that exists in these places is exemplified by the bustling bazaars, historical monuments, and thriving arts scenes that are found there. This culture successfully navigates between tradition and modernity.

A significant factor that has contributed to the heterogeneity of Afghanistan's national identity is the geographical diversity of the country's urban centers, each of which possesses its own distinct cultural history. The adaptability and resilience of the Afghan character in the face of changing circumstances is demonstrated by the country's capacity to strike a balance between the maintenance of traditional values and the requirements of a world that is undergoing fast technological advancement.

Struggle and Resilience: Finding Your Way Through Challenging Times

In times of peace, the demographic characteristics of Afghanistan have not only played a significant role in shaping the personality of the country's inhabitants, but they have also been a defining component in times of strife. In the past, the rugged landscape served as a natural bulwark against invaders. However, it has now become the backdrop for decades of conflict, with the Afghan people being caught in the crossfire.

The resiliency that is instilled in the Afghan character has been put to the test numerous times throughout the course of the conflict. The tenacity of the Afghan people is demonstrated by their capacity to adjust to shifting conditions, whether it is through the use of guerrilla warfare in the mountains or through the success-ful navigation of the complexity of geopolitical challenges. In more recent times, the geographical barriers that have traditionally acted as a defense mechanism have evolved into arenas for exhibiting a resilience that goes beyond the physical landscape.

The character of Afghanistan is a beautiful tapestry of resiliency, flexibility, and a profound connection to the land. This character is carefully sculpted by the geo-graphical elements of Afghanistan.

The steep terrain, dry plains, cultural crossroads, tribal structures, urban centers, and the hardships of conflict have all contributed to a national character that is as diverse as the landscapes that characterize the country. This character has been maintained throughout the country's history.

The people of Afghanistan have a spirit that has been able to withstand the stresses of time and the challenges that come from the outside world. This spirit was fashioned in the crucible of their difficult topography. The mountains, valleys, and plains of Afghanistan have not only given physical limits but have become vital aspects in the narrative of a people who have handled the complexity of their environment with unshakable tenacity. As Afghanistan continues to develop in the 21st century, it is essential to have a solid awareness of the dynamic relationship that exists between the country's personality and its geographical location in order to have a comprehension of the essence of a nation that is robust in the face of the shifting currents of history.

1.2 Cultural diversity and its impact on resilience

Cultural variety, which may be thought of as the rich tapestry that is spun by the myriad of human experiences, traditions, and expressions, is an essential component in the process of how societies are able to remain resilient. In the complicated nexus between cultural variety and resilience, where the amalgamation of many viewpoints, values, and traditions becomes a wellspring of strength in the face of adversities, this is nowhere more clear than it is in the complex relationship between the two. The purpose of this essay is to investigate the enormous impact that cultural diversity has on resilience. Specifically, the study will investigate how the celebration of differences can build flexibility, fortitude, and a collective power that is unaffected by resistance.

Recognizing and Appreciating Individual Differences: The Essence of Cultural Diversity

A fundamental aspect of cultural diversity is the recognition and appreciation of the distinctions that exist between people. It incorporates a wide range of aspects, such as ethnicity, language, religion, traditions, and customs, among others, while not being confined to these categories. When individuals and communities cohabit in societies that are defined by cultural diversity, they do so with the understanding that their particular histories contribute to the richness of the collective identity.

Rather than being a passive acknowledgment, the embrace of diversity transforms into an active celebration of the immense variety of ways in which people express themselves. Whether it be through the mediums of art, music, language, or religious rituals, cultural variety encompasses the spirit of pluralism. It helps to cultivate an atmosphere in which different points of view are not only tolerated but also embraced.

Cultural Resilience: Fostering Adaptability and Creativity of Individuals and Communities

Cultural diversity acts as a stimulant for flexibility and innovation, contributing to the development of resilience and serving as a crucible for the development of resilience. When a society is made up of people who come from a variety of different backgrounds, it naturally produces a pool of different experiences and methods to problem-solving. A pool of resilience is created as a result of this diversity of thought, which enables communities to address difficulties from a variety of perspectives.

Despite the challenges they encounter, cultures that are rich in cultural diversity frequently exhibit a remarkable capacity for adaptation and innovation. Individuals that are a part of such communities are able to handle complex situations with a versatility that is the result of the amalgamation of many cultural influences. This versatility is a result of drawing on a multitude of traditions, knowledge systems, and ways of thinking.

Take, for instance, a community that is struggling with environmental issues or problems. It is possible for a group that is culturally diverse to bring together traditional ecological knowledge from a range of various backgrounds. This approach can provide a comprehensive understanding of the environment as well as unique solutions that are rooted in a diversity of experiences. This adaptability, which is a result of the cross-fertilization of ideas, becomes a defining characteristic of cultural resilience.

Building Social Cohesion and Bridging Divides

The cultural diversity of a civilization serves as a bridge, linking the various components that make up that society. The development of social cohesion, which serves as a key component of resilience, can be accomplished by societies through the cultivation of an atmosphere in which diversity are not only recognized but also respected. The strengthening of social links, which in turn creates a foundation upon which communities may weather storms together, occurs when individuals from varied backgrounds have a sense of inclusion and are appreciated.

The importance of maintaining social cohesion cannot be overstated during times of crises. Whether they are dealing with natural disasters, economic downturns, or health emergencies, communities that have developed strong social links via cultural variety are better positioned to deploy collective resources. This is true regardless of the source of the crisis. The sense of common identity that develops as a result of recognizing and appreciating differences becomes a force that is capable of bringing people together regardless of the obstacles they face.

Furthermore, cultural variety brings about the dismantling of preconceptions and stereotypes, which in turn helps to tear down obstacles that would otherwise prevent cooperation.

The realization that resiliency is a collaborative activity, in which every voice matters, is pervasive among cultures that cherish and enjoy the various cultural tapestries that they possess.

The importance of cultural heritage as a wellspring of power and individuality

The complex tapestry of legacy constitutes the embodiment of cultural diversity. legacy is the practices, rituals, and traditions that have been handed down from generation to generation. This cultural history becomes a source of strength and identity, providing communities with a sense of stability during times of uncertainty and a road map for navigating change.

It is an act of resilience in and of itself to commit to the preservation of cultural legacy, whether it is through the use of language, the recounting of stories, or artistic forms. Communities that appreciate and protect their heritage exhibit a remarkable capacity to persevere, whether they are confronted with challenges from the outside world or they are experiencing the erosion of their cultural identity.

As an illustration, the transmission of indigenous knowledge from one generation to the next might be considered a sort of cultural resilience. In the fields of agriculture, medicine, and environmental stewardship, traditional practices embody within them the accumulated wisdom of communities. These traditions offer solutions that are sustainable and have withstood the test of time.

Catalysts for resilient societies are creativity and innovation

Diversity in cultural practices serves as a stimulant for creative and innovative thinking, both of which are key components of resilience in a world that is constantly changing. Creativity is sparked when diverse points of view collide, and this happens when they are fostered in an environment that embraces individuals' differences. When different cultural influences interact with one another in a dynamic way, it can become a source of fresh ideas and ways to problem-solving.

The individuals who live in cultures that are rich in cultural diversity draw inspiration from a variety of traditions, modifying and synthesizing notions in order to come up with original solutions. This method, which is anchored in the cross-pollination of many cultural backgrounds, becomes a driving force for creativity since it is interdisciplinary.

Take for example the fields of arts and sciences, which are areas in which originality is of the utmost importance. Culturally diverse communities frequently produce ground-breaking ideas, artworks, and scientific discoveries.

This is due to the fact that individuals bring distinctive viewpoints that are influenced by their experiences in their respective cultures. Through the cultivation of the capacity to conceive of and carry out transformative change, this creativity, which is woven into the very fabric of cultural diversity, moves societies toward resilience.

When it comes to navigating the complexities of diversity, there are both challenges and opportunities

It is necessary to acknowledge that the path is not devoid of difficulties, despite the fact that cultural diversity unquestionably adds to resilience. To successfully navigate the complexities of multiple perspectives, it is necessary to make conscious efforts to cultivate inclusivity, encourage dialogue, and address systemic injustices throughout the process.

There is a possibility that discrepancies will arise in terms of access to resources, representation, and opportunity in societies that are diverse. The process of recognizing and addressing these imbalances becomes an essential component in the process of maximizing the potential for resilience that cultural variety possesses. The development of a society that is more egalitarian and resilient can be facilitated by the implementation of policies that encourage inclusiveness, educational programs that honor diversity, and venues that facilitate intercultural discourse.

Furthermore, there is a requirement for a deep awareness of cultural variety that goes beyond actions that are only symbolic on the surface. When individuals are given the ability to bring their complete selves into the fabric of society and contribute their own points of view without the fear of being marginalized or discriminated against, true resilience emerges.

A tale of resiliency that transcends boundaries and celebrates differences is woven across the kaleidoscope of human experiences and manifestations that is cultural variety. The impact of cultural variety on resilience is significant, as it helps to cultivate adaptation, fortitude, and a collective strength that develops from the celebration of different points of view.

It is impossible to overestimate the significance of cultural diversity in the process of constructing resilience during the process of societies navigating the challenges of the 21st century. Whether it be in the face of global crises such as climate change, pandemics, or socio-economic inequities, the capacity to draw into the wide well of human experiences becomes an asset that is of incalculable value.

Not only do communities recognize the richness of their legacy when they celebrate cultural diversity, but they also put themselves at the forefront of resilience, ready to meet the uncertainties of a world that is constantly changing with the strength that develops from the unity that exists within differences.

Chapter 2

Invaders and Resistance

There are many instances in which the pages of history are imprinted by the footprints of invaders who were seeking sovereignty over overseas territories. A rival story of persistent resistance arises alongside the stories of conquering and imperial ambitions. Nevertheless, this narrative is equally important. An examination of the dynamics of power, resiliency, and the unconquerable spirit of people who stood against the tide of foreign dominance is the focus of this article, which unfolds the historical tapestry of invaders and resistance.

The Ancient Chronicles: Conquests and the Violent Resistance of Indigenous Peoples

Tales of invasion and resistance have been passed down through the decades, and they originate from the chronicles of ancient history. The conquests of empires such as the Assyrians, Persians, and Romans lay the groundwork for a pattern that would continue to exist for centuries: the conflict between the growth of imperial power and the resistance of indigenous peoples.

Throughout the history of the ancient world, conquerors frequently attempted to incorporate the cultures, faiths, and modes of government that they had brought with them into the lands that they had conquered. On the other hand, these initiatives were met with vehement opposition from groups who were unwilling to give up their independence. The Jewish Revolt against Roman control in the first century CE and the ongoing struggles of numerous city-states against the Persian Empire are two examples that illustrate the spirit of defiance that existed in ancient times.

There was a recurrent theme that emerged from the resistance, which was founded on a profound connection to ancestral lands and cultural identity. Native American communities, when confronted with the possibility of being dominated by outsiders, rose up to defend their traditional way of life. A legacy that would survive across civilizations and epochs was established through the connected narratives of invaders and resistance in the ancient world. These narratives laid the framework for the legacy.

The Battleground of the Middle Ages: Empires, Crusades, and the Valor of Indigenous Peoples

It was throughout the course of the medieval period that new invaders appeared on the international stage.

The conflict between those who conquered and those who were conquered had been going on for centuries, but the Islamic conquests, the Mongol invasions, and the Crusades brought up a new set of dynamics. At the forefront of the drama was the collision of cultures, with each side claiming their right to dominate the situation.

The Islamic conquests, particularly the expansions of the Umayyad and Abbasid empires, were met with opposition from other empires, including the Byzantine and Sasanian empires. The unyielding resistance of the Byzantine Empire, particularly during the Arab-Byzantine Wars, served as a prime example of the tenacity with which native nations maintained their lands against inroads from foreign powers.

The Mongol invasions, which were led by individuals such as Genghis Khan and Timur, left a pattern of destruction over the continents of Asia and Europe. Nevertheless, they, too, were confronted with insurmountable opposition from civilizations that were adamant about maintaining their autonomy. A sign of indigenous bravery in the face of tremendous circumstances, the Battle of Ain Jalut, which took place in 1260 and saw the Mamluks successfully repel the Mongols, became a symbol of indigenous valor.

Religious zeal and European expansionism were the driving causes behind the Crusades, which resulted in a conflict between Western soldiers and their Muslim counterparts. Despite the fact that the Crusaders were successful in capturing certain lands, the opposition that was put up by Muslim leaders such as Saladin and indigenous communities demonstrated the complexity of the relationship between the invaders and the resistance.

Colonialism and the Resistance of Indigenous Peoples During the Age of Exploration

In the long and winding story of invaders and resistance, the Age of Exploration marked the beginning of a new chapter. European nations, motivated by the aspiration to amass wealth and expand their territories, set sail on expeditions that would result in the redrawing of the world map. The colonization of the Americas, Africa, and Asia became a distinguishing characteristic of this century, and it laid the groundwork for intense fights for power and autonomy.

A significant cultural collision occurred in the Americas as a result of the interaction between European conquerors and the indigenous civilizations that existed there. The resistance of Native American tribes, which was exemplified by leaders such as Tecumseh and the numerous uprisings against the invasion of Europeans, became a powerful symbol of defiance. The stories of Pocahontas, the Pequot War, and the Aztec resistance led by personalities such as Cuauhtémoc highlighted the indigenous people's willingness to fight against the dominance of foreign powers.

On the African continent, the colonization of enormous territory was a direct result of the imperialistic aspirations of European nations. Nevertheless, the opposition against the control of colonial powers was unrelenting. Characters such as Samori Ture, Yaa Asantewaa, and Menelik II came to be seen as emblems of African resistance against European colonizers throughout history. Strong evidence of the resilience of indigenous resistance may be seen in the Battle of Adwa, which took place in 1896 and resulted in Ethiopian forces achieving a significant victory over Italian forces.

The colonization endeavors of European powers in Asia were met with opposition from a variety of different individuals and groups. There are many different types of indigenous resistance against colonial powers, and some examples include the Sepoy Mutiny in India, the Boxer Rebellion in China, and the campaigns for independence in Southeast Asia, such as the resistance of the Viet Minh against the French.

The World Wars: Occupations and Partisan Conflicts

In the form of two world wars, the 20th century witnessed the occurrence of global conflicts that had never been seen before. During these wars, occupations and invasions took place, and as a result, there were strong resistance movements against repressive regimes. Indigenous peoples that defied foreign rulers and occupiers took the occupied lands and turned them into battlegrounds for their resistance organizations.

Through the course of World War I, numerous territories were occupied, and in reaction, resistance movements came into existence. The Arab Revolt against Ottoman control, which was spearheaded by personalities such as T.E. Lawrence (Lawrence of Arabia), demonstrated the determination of native communities to break free from the restraints of imperial rule.

Resistance movements were observed all over Europe and Asia during World struggle II, which was characterized by its expansive theaters of struggle. Examples of populations that were able to persevere in the face of Nazi occupation include the French Resistance, the Polish Home Army, and the Yugoslav Partisans in Europe. It was in Asia that the Chinese resistance against Japanese aggression, the Filipino guerrilla warfare against the Japanese, and the efforts of the Indian National Army against British control brought to light the worldwide extent of the invaders and the resistance dynamic.

In the era of the Cold War, proxy wars and national liberation movements were prevalent

The ideological conflict that characterized the Cold War, which resulted in proxy wars and national liberation movements, was a defining characteristic of the period that followed World War II.

The resistance against what was considered to be interference from foreign powers and the invasions carried out by superpowers became essential components of this geopolitical landscape.

During the prolonged struggle in Vietnam, which was initially fought against French forces and then subsequently by American forces, the Vietnamese people proved their desire to fight back against foreign occupation. A determined fight that ultimately resulted in the reunification of Vietnam was represented by figures such as Ho Chi Minh and the Viet Cong, who became icons of this resistance.

There was a ferocious struggle from a variety of Mujahideen factions in Afghanistan in response to the Soviet invasion that took place in 1979. The Afghan people, drawing on their long tradition of resiliency, participated in guerrilla warfare against the armies of the Soviet Union. The conflict not only became a symbol of local resistance, but it also attracted actors from all over the world, establishing a new chapter in the tale of individuals who invaded and those who resisted.

Occupation, terrorism, and asymmetric warfare are the contemporary struggles that are being discussed

New complexity has been introduced into the interplay between invaders and resistance as a result of the 21st century. Following the terrorist attacks that occurred on September 11, 2001, the United States of America and its allies began conducting military operations in Afghanistan and Iraq as part of the War on Terror. As a result of the succeeding insurgencies and asymmetric warfare, resistance movements against foreign occupiers experienced a return to their previous level of activity.

The United States invasion of Iraq in 2003 was met with a varied resistance that included both indigenous groupings and foreign fighters. This resistance was met with conflict. It was difficult to differentiate between local resistance, sectarian strife, and foreign terrorism due to the complexity of the fight, which underlined the difficulties involved there.

The tenacity of the Afghan resistance was on full display during the protracted struggle in Afghanistan, which was initially conducted by the Soviets and later by a coalition led by the United States. The Mujahideen resistance eventually gave birth to the Taliban, which went on to become a strong entity in the struggle against what was believed to be foreign occupation.

Regarding the Israeli-Palestinian conflict, the quest for self-determination has been a recurring theme throughout the conflict.

Both armed and political resistance have been carried out by the resistance movements, which include organizations such as Hamas and Hezbollah, against those who are believed to be occupying the territory.

The current dynamic of invaders and resistance has also witnessed non-state actors utilizing asymmetric measures, including terrorism, in order to fight what they perceive to be the control of foreign powers. These resistance movements have spawned questions about the nature of terrorism and the validity of unconventional tactics in the face of overwhelming military might. These debates have been sparked by the motivations, techniques, and effects of these resistance groups.

Reflections and Lessons: Invaders, Resistance, and the Complicated Nature of Power

The historical interaction between invaders and resistance provides instructive and thought-provoking insights into the complexity of power, sovereignty, and the unconquerable spirit of the human race. What are some important factors to consider?

The disintegration of empires: The lessons of history demonstrate that no empire is protected from opposition. In the past, the most powerful forces have been met by opposition from individuals who are adamant about protecting their independence. Both the rise and fall of empires serve to highlight the ephemeral nature of power as well as the resiliency that is woven into the fabric of many communities.

There is a lot of ambiguity around the motivations that drive invasions and resistance movements. These motivations frequently involve multiple factors. Resistance is typically fuelled by a desire for self-determination, the preservation of cultural identity, or opposition to perceived injustices. Invaders may cite geopolitical, economic, or ideological motives for their actions; yet, resistance is frequently fueled by these desires. For a full comprehension of the dynamics of conflict, it is essential to have a solid understanding of the underlying motivations.

As a result of the complexity of asymmetric warfare, the present terrain of invaders and resistance is characterized by asymmetric warfare. This type of warfare is characterized by the use of unconventional strategies by non-state actors against significant state entities. Due to this asymmetry, it becomes difficult to define the boundaries of legal resistance, particularly in situations where strategies like as terrorism blur the boundary between political violence and civilian targeting.

Globalization of Resistance: In a world that is increasingly interconnected, resistance movements frequently extend beyond the borders of individual nations.

Alliances, support networks, and the internationalization of conflicts have emerged as a result of the global response to what is considered to be attempts at foreign involvement. This globalization of resistance brings forth new aspects to the dynamic between the invaders and the resistance, which has ramifications for both international politics and security.

The Imperative of Diplomacy and negotiation: While resistance may emerge through armed struggle, diplomacy and negotiation remain key components of conflict resolution. The historical record provides examples of situations in which negotiated agreements have resulted in the cessation of foreign occupations and the reestablishment of self-governance.

The narrative of invaders and resistance wove a rich tapestry of human history, symbolizing the ongoing battle for autonomy, identity, and justice. This narrative is woven into the fabric of human history. The conflict between those who desire domination and those who reject foreign intrusion has been a significant factor in the development of nations and civilizations throughout history, from the ancient civilizations to the modern geopolitical situation we find ourselves in today.

When this historical tapestry is examined, it becomes clear that the dynamics of invaders and resistance are complex, and they change over time in accordance with the ebb and flow of geopolitical currents. The stories of defiance, tenacity, and the pursuit of self-determination reverberate throughout time and cultures, serving as a reminder of the unconquerable spirit that develops when communities confront the shadow of foreign dominance.

Lessons from history provide useful insights into the complexity of power, the reasons that drive both invaders and resistance groups, and the need of finding diplomatic solutions to lengthy conflicts. These lessons are particularly relevant at a time when the globe is grappling with modern difficulties and conflicts. As far as the narrative of invaders and resistance is concerned, it is not a relic of the past; rather, it continues to influence the fate of nations and communities, leaving an indelible impression on the continuous saga of human resiliency and the desire of freedom.

2.1 Historical overview of foreign invasions

Invasions from other countries are a recurrent theme that has played a significant role in determining the fates of nations and civilizations throughout history. These invasions are intricately woven into the fabric of history. The chronicles of human history bore witness to a persistent ebb and flow of conquerors seeking dominion and indigenous populations rising up in defiance during the course of human history, beginning with the ancient world and continuing into the current age. This historical review dives into the eras of foreign invasions, investigating the patterns, motivations, and enduring legacies that have arisen as a result of the intricate interaction between those who conquered and those who were conquered.

Ancient conquests are considered to be the cradle of civilization

The ancient world was the birthplace of civilization, and it was there that the development of powerful empires occurred. Each of these empires left an unmistakable impact on the world through their conquests and expansions. In the region of Mesopotamia, which is frequently referred to as the "Fertile Crescent," civilizations such as the Akkadian, Babylonian, and Assyrian came into being. In order to construct one of the first and most powerful empires, the Assyrians, who were renowned for their military strength, participated in a series of invasions.

During the reign of Cyrus the Great, Egypt, which was a stronghold of ancient culture, was subjected to invasions by civilizations such as the Hyksos and, subsequently, the Persians. The Persians, on the other hand, expanded their empire by acquiring territories that extended beyond Asia Minor and into neighboring regions. The geopolitical environment underwent further transformation as a result of Alexander the Great's conquests, which resulted in the creation of the Hellenistic world, which encompassed the whole region from Greece to the Indian subcontinent.

The Roman Empire was a mighty empire that expanded through military conquests and the integration of various cultures. The ancient Mediterranean world was a witness to this expansion. Roman legions marched over Europe, North Africa, and the Middle East, bringing enormous territories under Roman power. This was accomplished by marching across these regions. On the other hand, even Rome, when it was at the height of its power, was confronted with opposition from tribes such as the Germanic peoples, who were adamantly opposed to the dominance of foreign powers.

The Conflicts of the Middle Ages: Empires, Crusades, and Nomadic Invasions

There was a rich tapestry of invasions that began during the medieval period. These invasions were characterized by the growth of empires, religious wars, and nomadic raids. In the course of their expansion across the Middle East, North Africa, and into Europe, the Islamic conquests, which were commanded by the Rashidun and Umayyad Caliphates, ran with opposition from Byzantine armies and European regions.

Under the leadership of Genghis Khan and his successors, the Mongol invasions resulted in the establishment of one of the largest contiguous empires in the history of the world. A wake of destruction was left behind by the Mongols as they stormed throughout Asia, Eastern Europe, and the Middle East. However, the Pax Mongolica served to facilitate cultural contact among the people of these regions.

An example of the collision of civilizations that occurred in the medieval era was the Crusades, which were a series of religious conflicts that were fought between Christian and Muslim forces. Multiple crusades were launched by European nations in an effort to regain the Holy Land, and Jerusalem became a focal point of conflict and conflict resolution. Not only did the Crusades result in changes to physical boundaries, but they also left behind a legacy of cultural and religious problems with their legacy.

The Age of Exploration: Colonization and Interactions with Indigenous Peoples

There was a fresh wave of foreign invasions that occurred during the Age of Exploration, which occurred between the 15th and 16th centuries. These invasions were fueled by marine exploration, economic goals, and territorial expansion. A number of European powers, most notably Spain, Portugal, Britain, France, and the Netherlands, set sail on expeditions that ultimately resulted in the colonization of the Americas, Africa, and Asia.

The interactions that took place between European conquerors and indigenous cultures in the Americas had a significant impact on the development of historic events. In their pursuit of wealth in the Aztec and Inca empires, respectively, the conquistadors, which included Hernán Cortés and Francisco Pizarro, were responsible for the subjugation and decimation of the native inhabitants. There were also conflicts that occurred between European settlers and Native American tribes during the process of colonization of North America, which resulted in a legacy of displacement and resistance.

The Scramble for Africa, which was a competition between European nations for control of Africa, led to the subdivision and colonization of the continent. The indigenous resistance movement, which was led by individuals such as Samori Ture, Yaa Asantewaa, and Menelik II, aimed to protect African sovereignty and fight back against the expansion of European powers.

The European powers built trade routes and colonies in Asia, and as a result, areas in India, Southeast Asia, and the Far East came under the control of foreign nations. The economic incentives behind these invasions were brought to light by things like the East India Company's dominion over some regions of the Indian subcontinent and the Opium Wars that took place in China.

Confrontations of the 20th Century: World Wars and Occupations on the World Stage

During the 20th century, there were two terrible world wars, each of which was characterized by invasions, occupations, and resistance movements from other countries. As a result of the collapse of empires during World War I, notably the Ottoman, Austro-Hungarian, and Russian empires, power vacuums were created, and state borders were redrawn.

Under the mandate system established by the League of Nations in the aftermath of World War I, colonial countries were given the responsibility of administering territory that had been previously held by defeated empires. While the mandates were purportedly intended to prepare regions for self-governance, they frequently resulted in ongoing foreign rule and resistance from the populations that were indigenous to the territories.

The Axis powers occupied a great number of countries during World War II, which took place across the globe in the various theaters of conflict. Invasion of Europe by the Nazis, expansion of Japan into Asia, and the establishment of collaborationist regimes all contributed to the formation of intricate dynamics of foreign domination and resistance. From France to the Philippines, occupied territories were battlegrounds for partisan warfare and underground movements. These territories included the Philippines.

As a result of ideological conflicts, the Cold War proxy conflicts

The United States of America and the Soviet Union engaged in an ideological confrontation during the time period known as the Cold War, which resulted in proxy wars and interventions from other countries. In both the Korean War and the Vietnam War, which were both founded in the containment of communism, there were invasions from other countries and opposition from the native population.

The Korean Peninsula became a battlefield during the Cold War as a result of the struggle that took place in Korea between North and South Korea due to the involvement of foreign forces. During the Vietnam War, which was defined by the intervention of the United States against the troops of the Viet Cong and North Vietnam, there was a prolonged struggle for independence and reunification.

Globalization and asymmetric warfare are two contemporary challenges that cannot be ignored

The latter half of the 20th century and the beginning of the 21st century brought about the introduction of new difficulties and complications to the dynamics of invasions from other countries. As a result of globalization, technical improvements, and asymmetric warfare, the character of hostilities has been significantly altered.

Following the terrorist attacks that occurred on September 11, 2001, the United States of America and its allies began conducting military operations in Afghanistan and Iraq as part of the War on Terror. During the course of these conflicts, prolonged occupations, insurgencies, and resistance groups were launched against what were seen to be foreign occupiers.

The war between Israel and the Palestinians in the Middle East is still characterized by interventions by outside parties, geographical disputes, and resistance from the Palestinian people. The persistent character of invasions and resistance is demonstrated by the complexity of this struggle, which have their origins in historical grudges and geopolitical rivalry.

Additional complexities are added to the terrain of foreign interventions by the presence of cyber warfare and non-state entities. As a means of pushing back against what is considered to be foreign dominance, asymmetric strategies, including terrorism, have emerged as effective instruments. Defining the nature of disputes and legitimizing resistance movements can be difficult due to the blurred lines that exist between state actors and non-state players.

The historical review of invasions from other countries reveals a complex web of conquest, resistance, and the complicated interplay of power relations. There is a consistent narrative of invaders and resistance throughout the entirety of human history, from the ancient civilizations of Mesopotamia to the modern difficulties of the 21st century. This narrative is a distinguishing characteristic of human history.

Resistance movements have evolved as demonstrations of the indomitable human spirit, a drive to defend autonomy, culture, and identity. Invasion attempts have resulted in the redrawing of maps, the alteration of destiny, and the imposition of foreign rule. There have been a variety of reasons for invasions, ranging from economic interests and territorial expansion to ideological fights. On the other hand, resistance has frequently been motivated in the pursuit of self-determination, justice, and the preservation of legacy.

As the world continues to suffer with hostilities, geopolitical tensions, and fights for autonomy, the lessons that may be learned from the historical tapestry of invasions from other countries continue to maintain their relevance. In order to successfully navigate the obstacles that come with a dynamic and interconnected global landscape, it is vital to have a solid understanding of the complexity of power, the reasons that drive invasions and resistance, and the urgency of finding diplomatic solutions. In this ongoing saga of conquest and defiance, the echoes of history serve as guides for constructing a future that seeks harmony, fairness, and a respect for the sovereignty of nations. This narrative is ongoing.

2.2 Patterns of resistance against various conquerors

The chronicle of humanity has been distinguished not only by the conquests of empires and foreign forces throughout history, but also by the stubborn spirit of individuals who fought foreign domination. This has been the case throughout the course of human history. A rich tapestry is created by the patterns of resistance against many invaders. This tapestry weaves together stories of bravery, persistence, and the unyielding pursuit of freedom. This investigation digs into the recurrent patterns of resistance that have surfaced throughout a variety of cultures, geographies, and eras, demonstrating the unconquerable spirit of the human race in the face of alien dominance.

The Violent Resistance of Native Peoples in Ancient Civilizations

Indigenous inhabitants frequently found themselves at the forefront of struggle against foreign conquerors in the cradle of civilization, which was a place where empires rose and fell. It was the Babylonians, the Medes, and other regional powers that put up a fight against the Assyrians, who were known for their considerable military force. For instance, the Chaldean king Nabopolassar was the leader of a victorious rebellion against the Assyrians. This rebellion was the first in a series of indigenous uprisings.

In ancient Egypt, foreign rulers such as the Hyksos meet fierce opposition from native pharaohs who seek to remove the invaders and restore Egyptian sovereignty. These native pharaohs were looking to restore Egyptian sovereignty. The New Kingdom, which was characterized by the expulsion of the Hyksos, is a prime example of the desire of indigenous leaders to fight imperial rule and restore their properties.

One of the most striking examples of religious and cultural resistance is the Jewish Revolts, which were directed against foreign domination. The Maccabean Revolt, which took place in the second century BCE against the Seleucid Empire, and the Great Jewish Revolt, which took place in the first century CE against the

Roman Empire, both highlighted the fierce struggle of the Jewish people against attempts to repress their religious and cultural identity.

Empires, Crusaders, and Nomadic Incursions: The Development of Resistance During the Middle Ages

During the medieval period, there was a convergence of empires, religious disputes, and nomadic incursions, all of which were greeted with different kinds of resistance. An example of a coordinated resistance against foreign troops was demonstrated by the Islamic world during their conflict with the Crusaders. During the Third Crusade, figures such as Saladin became icons of resistance against Western encroachment. They were responsible for rallying Muslim armies as they attempted to regain Jerusalem.

Despite the fact that the Mongol invasions were notorious for their destruction, they were met with resistance from a variety of cultures. During the Battle of Ain Jalut, which took place in 1260, the Mamluks secured a major victory over the Mongols. This victory demonstrated that even the troops who appeared to be unstoppable could be met with effective opposition by the indigenous people.

Over the course of its existence in India, the Delhi Sultanate encountered recurrent opposition from provincial rulers and local communities. For example, the Vijayanagara Empire developed into a powerful Hindu monarchy that was able to withstand the invasions of the Delhi Sultanate.

During the Colonial Era, Indigenous Peoples Fought Against the Process of Colonization

The Age of Exploration marked the beginning of the colonization era, which brought European powers into touch with a wide variety of cultures across the Americas, Africa, and Asia. Native American communities were confronted with the issue of putting up a fight against foreign conquerors who were attempting to impose their authority and extract resources.

There were Native American tribes in the Americas that fought against European colonialism by armed combat, diplomatic maneuvering, and adaptation. Individuals such as Powhatan, who lived in North America, as well as the leaders of the Aztec and Inca civilizations, who lived in Mesoamerica, endeavored to protect their territories and cultures against the European powers that were advancing on them.

There were many different manifestations of resistance to colonization in Africa. Leaders such as Samori Ture in West Africa, Menelik II in Ethiopia, and Yaa Asantewaa in the Ashanti Empire displayed the determination to defend African sovereignty against the imperialistic aspirations of Europeans.

Resistance movements were generated throughout Asia as a result of the colonial operations brought about by European powers. The Sepoy Mutiny in India, the Boxer Rebellion in China, and the Philippine Revolution against Spanish and subsequently American control are all examples of the various ways in which indigenous populations have resisted the dominance of foreign powers.

In the face of conquest, defiance is displayed during the world wars and occupations

There were two world wars that occurred throughout the 20th century, which resulted in international occupations, invasions, and resistance movements affecting the entire world. The regions that were occupied became arenas for indigenous people to demonstrate their rebellion against tyrannical administrations.

In the course of World War II, occupied Europe was the scene of countless incidents of resistance against the ruling Nazi regime. The bravery of locals who resisted foreign occupation through covert operations, sabotage, and underground networks was highlighted by movement groups such as the French Resistance, the Polish Home Army, and partisan forces in Yugoslavia.

There were a number of nations in Asia that had resistance activities as a result of the Japanese occupation. The Chinese resistance against Japanese aggression, the guerrilla warfare in the Philippines, and the efforts of the Indian National Army against British control are all examples of the diverse forms of resistance that may be found in the face of foreign occupation.

Proxy Wars and National Liberation During the Last Decade of the Cold War

During the time of the Cold War, there were ideological confrontations, proxy wars, and national liberation movements. During this time, indigenous communities fought against foreign involvement and imperialist aspirations.

The Viet Minh's battle against French colonial control in Vietnam, as well as its subsequent resistance against American forces during the Vietnam War, exemplified the power that indigenous movements had in the quest for self-determination. The Ho Chi Minh Trail, which consisted of a convoluted network of supply channels, exemplified the tenacity of resistance against an adversary who possessed superior technological capabilities.

The invasion of Afghanistan by the Soviet Union in 1979 sparked a prolonged resistance movement among the many different Mujahideen factions. Guerrilla warfare was waged against the Soviet army by the Afghan people, who drew on their long tradition of resistance. The conflict not only became a symbol of local resistance, but it also attracted actors from all over the world, establishing a new chapter in the tale of individuals who invaded and those who resisted.

Asymmetric warfare and non-state actors are one of the contemporary challenges that we face

Asymmetric warfare and the participation of non-state actors are two examples of the contemporary issues that have led to the development of new patterns of resistance in the 21st century. Following the terrorist attacks that occurred on September 11, 2001, the United States of America and its allies began conducting military operations in Afghanistan and Iraq as part of the War on Terror.

The United States invasion of Iraq in 2003 was met with a varied resistance that included both indigenous groupings and foreign fighters. This resistance was met with conflict. It was difficult to differentiate between local resistance, sectarian strife, and foreign terrorism due to the complexity of the fight, which underlined the difficulties involved there.

The tenacity of the Afghan resistance was on full display during the protracted struggle in Afghanistan, which was initially conducted by the Soviets and later by a coalition led by the United States. The Mujahideen resistance eventually gave birth to the Taliban, which went on to become a strong entity in the struggle against what was believed to be foreign occupation.

The current dynamic of resistance has also witnessed non-state actors utilizing asymmetric techniques, such as terrorism, in order to resist what they perceive to be the dominance of foreign powers. These resistance movements have spawned questions about the nature of terrorism and the validity of unconventional tactics in the face of overwhelming military might. These debates have been sparked by the motivations, techniques, and effects of these resistance groups.

A continuum of human history is formed by the patterns of resistance against numerous invaders. This continuum embodies the universal struggle for autonomy, dignity, and freedom. The unyielding willpower of individuals who fought against foreign domination has been a significant factor in the development of nations and civilizations throughout history, from the ancient civilizations to the modern problems of the 21st century.

There have been many different types of resistance throughout history, ranging from military revolutions and guerilla warfare to diplomatic maneuvering and cultural preservation. However, the fundamental concept has remained the same no matter what. Indigenous communities have persistently taken action to defend their territories, customs, and identities against the encroachments of conquerors. This is because indigenous peoples have been confronted with the notion of foreign dominance.

The lessons that may be learned from the patterns of resistance offer deep insights at a time when the globe is still struggling to deal with geopolitical tensions, conflicts, and battles for self-determination. By gaining an understanding of the historical subtleties of indigenous defiance, one can gain a roadmap for navigating present issues, cultivating empathy, and striving towards a future in which the dignity and sovereignty of every people are honored. The resilience of the human spirit in the face of hardship is demonstrated by the tapestry of resistance that has been woven through the years. This is a monument to the longevity of the human spirit.

Chapter 3

Tribal Dynamics

Since the beginning of time, tribal dynamics have been an integral component of human society. They have played a significant role in establishing the social, cultural, and political landscapes of communities, as well as shaping the fabric of communities. Tribes have been crucial in defining identities, maintaining traditions, and navigating the complexity of power hierarchies over a wide range of time periods and geographical locations. The purpose of this essay is to investigate the historical roots, cultural relevance, and modern ramifications of tribalism. It does so by delving into the complex world of tribal dynamics.

What are the historical origins of tribalism?

The origins of tribal dynamics can be traced back to the earliest human cultures. Primitive human societies are found around the world. In order to ensure their own survival in an environment that was more primitive, individuals organized themselves into tribes. Kinship bonds, shared areas, and collaborative efforts for hunting, gathering, and defense against external dangers were some of the characteristics that distinguished these early tribes.

In the course of the development of ancient civilizations, tribal systems continued to exist alongside the emergence of more sophisticated societal forms. Historically, ancient civilizations were frequently made up of a patchwork of many tribes, each of which had its own unique set of cultural practices, languages, and social standards. The diverse tribes that lived in Mesopotamia, the tribes of Israel that were mentioned in the biblical narrative, and the tribal societies that existed on the Indian subcontinent are all different examples.

The Importance of Tribes in Different Cultures:

Protecting Cultural Identity: Throughout history, tribes have been responsible for the preservation of distinct cultural identities. The transmission of language, rituals, folklore, and traditional customs from one generation to the next is a common occurrence within the setting of tribal communities. There is a sense of continuity and belonging that is fostered by the preservation of these cultural components, which also serves to anchor individuals to their Native American ancestry.

Tribal dynamics provide an emphasis on social cohesion and solidarity by highlighting the importance of these concepts. Because of the communal basis of tribal life, cooperation and mutual support are encouraged at all times.

A close-knit social fabric is created within the tribe as a result of shared tasks, such as communal agriculture or collective defense. These responsibilities reinforce the links that comprise the tribe.

Numerous indigenous communities incorporate spiritual beliefs and symbols into their cultural rituals, which gives them a significant spiritual and symbolic meaning. Sacred sites, totemic animals, and ceremonial rites all retain a great deal of significance, and they frequently serve as factors that bring members of a tribe together. Having these components contributes to a common worldview, which in turn helps to reinforce the distinct identity of the tribe.

Structures Used by Tribes and Their Governance:

Systems of Kinship: Kinship is an essential component of the structures that make up tribal societies. It is common for tribes to organize themselves according to the familial links that exist within them, with clans or extended family units serving as the fundamental components of social organization. Cultural norms including marriage, inheritance, and social roles are all impacted by the kinship system.

There are many different types of tribal organizations, and most of them have a hierarchical structure that is governed by elders or traditional leaders. These leaders, who frequently possess both wisdom and experience, serve as guides for the tribe in terms of decision-making and the resolution of conflicts. Respect for their culture and a commitment to the customs of their tribe are the foundations of their leadership.

Nomadic and Sedentary Tribes: The dynamics of a tribe change depending on whether or not the members of that tribe were nomadic or sedentary. The Bedouin people of the Arabian Desert and the Maasai people of East Africa are two examples of nomadic tribes that have developed distinctive social structures as a result of frequent movement. On the other hand, sedentary tribes might build more elaborate towns and agricultural methods than other tribes.

Power and Tribalism

The dynamics of tribal communities typically entail relationships with other tribes, which can lead to both conflict and cooperation. It is usual for people to work together for the purpose of mutual gain; nevertheless, rivalry over resources or territory can result in conflicts. In historical accounts, tribal warfare is frequently shown as a means by which tribes attempted to impose their control or safeguard their interests.

The influence of tribal dynamics extends to political systems, which gives rise to the phenomenon of tribalism.

Tribes can frequently serve as the foundation for political representation or power in certain contexts. This is especially clear in areas where tribal affiliations play a significant part in the institutions of government, which in turn influence political allegiances and the allocation of power.

The Obstacles That Tribalism Presents to Contemporary Nation-States:

Within the framework of contemporary nation-states, tribal dynamics have the potential to present difficulties for government. A number of considerations, including favoritism based on ethnicity or tribal affiliation, rivalry for resources, and the possibility of conflict between different tribes, are factors that policymakers need to handle. Finding a way to maintain cultural identities while yet encouraging national unity is a challenging endeavor that requires patience and deliberation.

Implications of Tribal Dynamics in the Present Day:

Globalization and the Identity of Tribal Communities Globalization has presented tribal communities with a variety of benefits as well as several obstacles. The conventional ways of life have been put in jeopardy, despite the fact that it has contributed to an increase in connectedness and made it easier for people to share their thoughts. The introduction of new influences from the outside can have an effect on the identities of tribal members and present difficulties in maintaining cultural customs.

Economic Shifts and Tribal Livelihoods: Economic changes, such as transitions from traditional subsistence economies to market-oriented systems, have substantial repercussions for the livelihoods of tribal communities. The expansion of industries, alterations in land usage, and the commercialization of resources have the potential to disrupt the traditional means of subsistence for a great number of indigenous communities.

Tribalism in the Digital era The advent of the digital era has both exacerbated and altered the social dynamics of tribal communities. There are platforms available for tribes to engage with one another and proclaim their identity, such as online communities, social media, and virtual places. On the other hand, this digital tribalism raises concerns about the possibility of echo chambers, polarization, and the dissemination of false information.

Rights of Indigenous Peoples and Activism Indigenous and tribal groups all over the world have been increasingly involved in activism in order to safeguard their rights, territories, and cultures. There is a modern battle among tribes to manage the complexity of a world that is changing at a rapid pace, and movements that advocate for indigenous rights, environmental conservation, and cultural preservation reflect this struggle.

Obstacles and Potential Opportunities:

Preservation of Cultural Diversity Despite the fact that tribal dynamics promote cultural diversity, there are problems that must be overcome in order to properly preserve different traditions. As a result of globalization, cultural homogenization, and other external forces, traditional customs may become less prevalent. There is an increasing importance placed on the documentation, revitalization, and transmission of indigenous cultures to subsequent generations.

Resolution of Conflict: Inter-tribal disputes, whether they are historical or modern, provide challenges to the maintenance of peace and security around the world. In order to effectively handle these difficulties, it is vital to put into place methods for dispute resolution that are both effective and respectful of tribal authority while simultaneously encouraging cooperation.

Empowerment and Representation: It is of the utmost importance to encourage the empowerment of tribal populations by providing them with access to education, economic possibilities, and representation in political processes. In order to contribute to societies that are more inclusive and equitable, it is important to make sure that the voices of tribal people are heard in areas that affect their lives.

In the field of environmental stewardship, numerous indigenous tribes have, for many generations, successfully maintained sustainable connections with their respective ecosystems. In order to make additional progress toward ecological sustainability, it is essential to acknowledge and support the environmental stewardship practices of indigenous communities.

3.1 Exploration of Afghan tribal structures

Afghanistan, a country that is located at the intersection of Central Asia and South Asia, is home to a diverse array of tribal institutions that have been essential in the manner in which the country's social, political, and cultural landscape has developed throughout the course of its history. The investigation of Afghan tribal structures reveals a complicated mosaic of interconnected communities, each of which possesses its own distinct identity, traditions, and governing systems. The purpose of this essay is to investigate the complex web of Afghan tribalism by analyzing its historical origins, cultural significance, and present relevance.

The Past Origins of the Tribal System in Afghanistan:

The origins of Afghan tribal structures can be traced back to ancient migrations and historical contacts. These migration patterns have been passed down through generations. The region has been witness to the migration of a wide variety of ethnic groups, including Pashtuns, Tajiks, Hazaras, Uzbeks, and others. The basis for the complex tribal landscape was set by these migrations, which were influenced by a variety of causes including commerce, invasions, and geographical features.

Pashtunwali Code: The Pashtunwali code is a traditional ethical code that is observed by Pashtun tribes. It is considered to be the most important aspect of Afghan tribalism. There are a number of guiding concepts that are included in Pashtunwali, including hospitality (melmastia), justice (nanawatai), and revenge (badal). Not only has this code played a large role in shaping Pashtun identity, but it has also had an impact on the broader tribal culture of Afghanistan.

The Religious and Cultural Importance of Afghan Tribes:

For the purpose of preserving their identities, Afghan tribes act as the guardians of their distinct cultural identities. The complex cultural tapestry of Afghanistan is a result of the fact that different tribes have different ways of speaking, dressing, and using customs. The maintenance of these identities is frequently regarded as a source of pride and a source of resilience in the face of impacts from their surroundings.

The foundation of Afghan tribal systems is composed of kinship ties, which are also the foundation of social cohesion. Clans and extended families are essential components of social structure because they foster a sense of belonging and provide support to everyone involved. Within the context of Afghanistan's frequently difficult and rocky terrain, this social connection is of the utmost importance.

Customs and Rituals of the Tribes: The Indian culture places a considerable emphasis on the importance of tribal rituals and customs. Particular occasions, such as weddings, celebrations, and religious rites, are occasions in which tribal identity is vividly shown. The relationships that exist within the tribe are strengthened as a result of these events, which also contribute to the continuity of cultural customs.

The Structures of Afghan Tribal Governments and Their Governance:

Jirgas and Shuras: Jirgas and shuras are two types of religious gatherings that are commonly used among Afghan tribes for the purpose of making traditional decisions. During these gatherings, tribe elders and leaders join together to discuss things of significance, find solutions to disagreements, and deliberate collectively on matters of importance. There is a strong connection between the authority of these meetings and the traditions of the tribe.

Maliks and Khans: Maliks and khans, as well as other recognized elders who possess influence and authority, are frequently entrusted with the responsibility of leadership within Afghan tribes. These leaders have critical responsibilities in the resolution of conflicts, the representation of the tribe in matters pertaining to the outside world, and the maintenance of tribal traditions. An individual's age, level of wisdom, and commitment to the rules of their tribe are the factors that contribute to the legitimacy of their leadership.

In the present day, Afghanistan faces a number of challenges and adaptations

The prolonged battles in Afghanistan, such as the Soviet-Afghan War, civil wars, and the War on Terror, have had a significant impact on the tribal structures that have been established as a result of these conflicts. In Afghanistan, the traditional cohesiveness of the tribes has been challenged by factors such as displacement, fragmentation, and the influence of actors from outside the country.

Tribalism in the Political Landscape The political landscape of Afghanistan has been intricately connected with the behaviors of many tribal groups. A number of political leaders, like Hamid Karzai, who served as President of Afghanistan in the past, have utilized tribal affiliations in order to attract support. The quest of political stability continues to be a struggle because it is difficult to strike a balance between the requirement for a centralized administration and the various tribal makeup.

The influence of other actors has resulted in the introduction of complications into the dynamics of Afghan tribal groups. These external actors include bordering countries and international entities. Tensions that already exist can be exacerbated by external forces, which can also upset established power structures and reshape local allegiances of individuals.

The dynamics of urbanization and change have brought about alterations to traditional tribal systems. Urbanization and modernity have brought about these changes. It is possible that the dynamics of tribal identity and allegiance will undergo modifications as younger generations move to metropolitan centers in search of greater educational opportunities and work opportunities. Maintaining a sense of tradition while meeting the requirements of a society that is always changing presents a difficult problem.

The Situation of Afghan Tribalism in the Future:

Contribution to Reconciliation and Stability: Afghan tribal systems have the potential to make a significant contribution to the pursuit of reconciliation and stability. It is possible to contribute to a peace process that is more inclusive and sustainable by acknowledging the legitimacy of tribal governance, adopting traditional conflict settlement procedures, and engaging tribal leaders in peace-building projects.

Maintaining Cultural Diversity As Afghanistan navigates its way through the future, it is becoming increasingly important to take measures to maintain cultural diversity within regional tribal communities. It is possible to contribute to the durability of Afghan cultural identities by providing support to efforts that document, promote, and conserve traditional practices.

Achieving a Balance Between Tradition and Modernity The problem that Afghanistan faces is to achieve a balance between the demands of modernity and the obligations of tradition. In order to assist bridge the gap between ancient tribal institutions and current realities, it is important to acknowledge the changing nature of Afghan society and to solicit the participation of younger generations in the process of building the future.

The investigation of Afghan tribal institutions reveals a story that is intricately connected to the history, culture, and difficulties of the country. The tenacity of Afghan tribes, their capacity to adjust to shifting conditions, and the significance they play in the administration of local affairs are all factors that highlight the persistent role that they play in the terrain of Afghanistan. Understanding the complexity of tribal dynamics and actively interacting with them will be vital for creating unity, peace, and a common sense of national identity in Afghanistan as the country continues to chart its route forward. The complex fabric of Afghan tribalism, which has been weaved through centuries of history, continues to determine the destiny of a nation that stands at the crossroads of tradition and modernization.

3.2 Role of tribal loyalties in resisting outside control

Tribal loyalties, which are strongly ingrained in cultural traditions and familial relationships, have played a vital part in crafting the narratives of resistance against outside rule over the course of history. The unbreakable links that exist among tribal societies have functioned as formidable barriers against the dominance of outside forces throughout history, from the earliest civilizations to the most recent contemporary conflicts. In this essay, the historical tapestry of tribal resistance is investigated. Specifically, the essay investigates how the strength of tribal loyalty has been a driving force in the face of foreign invasions, occupations, and attempts at control.

Ancient civilizations: protecting their homelands and heritage

Throughout the annals of ancient history, tribal affiliations have been seen as a formidable force that serves as a barrier to influence from other sources. The unwavering dedication of the Jewish tribes to the preservation of their religious identity and territory was demonstrated by their struggle against a variety of conquerors, including the Babylonians and the Romans. The fervor of the Maccabees during the Hellenistic period is a good example of how the strength of tribal relationships was able to sustain a prolonged struggle against overwhelming odds.

In a similar manner, the fight of the Germanic tribes against the expansionist ambitions of the

The Roman Empire demonstrated the significance of tribal loyalty in protecting ancestral territories and maintaining autonomy. It is a monument to the resiliency of tribes such as the Cherusci, who banded together against Roman raids, that the Battle of the Teutoburg Forest took place.

In the face of Crusaders and Mongols, tribal defiance was a source of conflict during the Middle Ages

In particular, regions that were characterized by Crusades and Mongol invasions at the time, tribal allegiance was an important factor in the process of fighting external forces during the medieval period. During the Crusaders' attempt to take control of Jerusalem in the Holy Land, Muslim armies formed tribal alliances with one another, which were based on their shared religious beliefs and cultural similarities. People like Saladin developed as leaders who were able to bring together various tribes for the purpose of achieving a common goal.

The Mongol invasions, which were characterized by an unprecedented level of savagery, were met with a ferocious resistance from many tribes, including the Mamluks in the Middle East and the Rus' in Eastern Europe. Despite their superior military capabilities, the Mongols had difficulties in capturing territories where tribal allegiances ran deep and local communities fiercely preserved their independence.

Colonial encounters: indigenous peoples who resisted imperialism aspirations

The period of exploration brought European colonial powers into contact with a wide variety of indigenous communities located in Asia, Africa, and the Americas from all over the world. Indigenous peoples banded together to defend their territories, customs, and ways of life, which resulted in the formation of tribal affiliations that became a strong force in the fight against imperial ambitions.

There was a concerted effort on the part of Native American tribes in North America to fight against European colonialism. Tribal alliances were formed in order to combat the settlers who were advancing. At the beginning of the 19th century, Tecumseh led a confederation that brought together a number of different tribes in opposition to westward expansion. This union demonstrated the power of tribal cohesion.

Both the Maasai and Zulu tribes in Africa put up a spirited fight against European colonization, yet there were distinct differences between the two groups. While the Zulu, led by individuals such as Shaka Zulu, participated in wars to maintain their independence, the Maasai adopted guerilla tactics against the British forces that were stationed in East Africa.

Occupied territories and the resistance of indigenous peoples during World Wars

Tribal resistance to foreign occupations was observed in a number of different theaters of warfare throughout the 20th century, which was distinguished by two consecutive world wars. The lands that were occupied turned into battlegrounds, where tribal allegiances served as the fuel for insurgencies and partisan fighting.

In Europe, during World War II, the French Resistance consisted of people who came from a variety of different backgrounds, including tribal ties, but they were united in their opposition to the occupation by the Nazi movement. The region of Ardennes, in which local resistance fighters played a significant role, served as a prime example of the efficacy of tribal loyalty in the face of outsider domination.

Both the Viet Minh in Vietnam and different partisan groups in Eastern Europe exhibited the persistent tenacity of tribal-like relationships in their resistance to Axis occupiers. Both of these organizations were located in Asia. There were hubs of resistance against foreign dominance that emerged from the interwoven networks of communities, villages, and tribes.

Struggles in the Post-Colonial Era: Tribal Identities and the Struggle for National Independence

The post-colonial era was marked by the development of new states, which were frequently influenced by the identities and allegiances of tribal groups. During the fight for independence, several communities fought to express their autonomy and maintain their cultural heritage. Tribal loyalties played a role in the struggle for freedom.

In the case of Algeria, for instance, the battle for independence from French colonial power overlapped with the tribal loyalties that existed within French Algeria. The National Liberation Front (FLN) included tribal networks into its battle against foreign rule, underlining the significance of tribe solidarity in the process of accomplishing national goals.

Contemporary Conflicts: The Resilience of Tribal Communities in the Face of Invasion

The ongoing importance that tribal affiliations play in the fight against foreign invasion and domination is highlighted by the battles that are taking place now, especially those that are taking place in Afghanistan and Iraq. There were tribal networks and local affiliations that served as the foundation for the Mujahideen's resistance in Afghanistan against the Soviet occupation. With each Pashtun tribe having its own unique identity, the intricate web of Pashtun tribes evolved into a formidable force that fought against outside authority.

In a similar manner, tribal loyalty were a crucial factor in the resistance movement in Iraq against the invasion and subsequent occupation by the United States. When it came to the Sunni insurgency in particular, tribal networks that were hostile to what they considered to be foreign rule provided the most support.

Obstacles and Difficulties: Striking a Balance Between National Unity and Tribal Identity

In spite of the fact that tribal loyalties have been shown to be rather resistant to control from outside sources, they also provide difficulties in terms of nation-building and governance. Especially in nations that have a diverse ethnic and tribal composition, striking a balance between the preservation of tribal identities and the promotion of national unity continues to be a difficult and delicate challenge.

The complex relationship that exists between tribal organizations and centralized authority in Afghanistan has been a source of both stability and discontent in the country until recently. When attempts have been made to form a powerful national government, they have frequently been met with opposition by tribes that are hesitant to abandon their autonomy.

The role that tribal loyalties have played in the process of rejecting authority from outside sources has been a thread that has been woven into the fabric of human history. Throughout history, tribes have served as pillars of resistance against the dominance of foreign powers, whether they were engaged in ancient civilizations, medieval hostilities, colonial encounters, or modern warfare. When confronted with demands from the outside world, the power that is generated from familial bonds, shared histories, and a profound connection to ancestral lands has repeatedly been shown to be an unstoppable force.

In order for policymakers, historians, and academics to successfully traverse the complexity of war and governance, it is vital for them to have a solid understanding of the dynamics of tribal opposition. However, despite the fact that they pose difficulties for central authorities, tribal loyalties are also a manifestation of the profound human need for autonomy, the preservation of cultural traditions, and the protection of collective identities. In a world that is characterized by fluctuating geopolitical landscapes, the historical tapestry of tribal resistance offers as a tribute to the enduring spirit of communities that are bound by the bonds of kinship and shared destiny.

Chapter 4

Guerrilla Warfare

One of the most distinguishing characteristics of wars throughout history has been the use of guerrilla warfare, which is distinguished by its unorthodox strategies and asymmetrical nature. The use of guerrilla warfare by non-state actors against conventional military forces has shown to be an effective technique throughout history, from the earliest civilizations to the most recent insurgencies. The purpose of this essay is to investigate the many facets of guerrilla warfare, including its historical roots, the development of tactics, its influence on conflicts, and the modern dynamics that continue to exert an influence on the nature of warfare.

The Historical Beginnings and Development of Guerrilla Warfare: From Ancient Times to Contemporary Guerrilla Violence

The origins of guerrilla warfare can be traced back to ancient times, when smaller, more mobile forces engaged in hit-and-run tactics against bigger, more conventional armies. This is where the tradition of guerrilla warfare originated. As an illustration, consider the strategies that the Numidian cavalry utilized in their conflict with the Roman legions during the Punic Wars, as well as the Partisan warfare that took place in the ancient Chinese state of Qi.

The modern concept of guerrilla warfare evolved during the Peninsular War (1808–1814), when Spanish irregular forces, known as guerrilleros, opposed Napoleon's occupation by deploying ambushes and hit-and-run tactics. This conflict took place in the 18th and 19th centuries. In a similar manner, during the American Civil War, irregulars from the Confederacy, who were frequently referred to as guerrillas, participated in unorthodox military strategies against Union forces.

During the 20th century, guerilla tactics were utilized extensively during both of the World Wars. This was a significant event that occurred during the 20th century. The effectiveness of irregular troops in repelling technologically superior foes was proved by partisan movements, such as the Yugoslav Partisans led by Tito, which were fighting against the seizure of the territories by the Nazis.

Guerrilla warfare is characterized by the following elements:

Ambushes, hit-and-run attacks, sabotage, and harassment are all examples of unconventional tactics that are utilized in guerrilla warfare. This type of warfare is distinguished by its dependence on unusual battle strategies.

A common strategy employed by irregular troops is to steer clear of direct clashes with conventional armies and instead concentrate on taking advantage of the weaknesses of their opponents.

Guerrilla forces are renowned for their mobility and adaptability, which are two of their most distinguishing characteristics. Their ability to quickly adjust to shifting conditions and terrain is facilitated by the fact that they function in small, decentralized groupings. This mobility not only increases their capacity to survive, but it also makes them difficult to capture by conventional forces that are larger and move more slowly.

Support from the Community and Insurgency: Guerrilla movements frequently flourish with the support of the community. They embed themselves within communities, relying on the populace for refuge, knowledge, and recruits. They also recruit potential members. This intimate relationship to the local populace makes it difficult for conventional forces to differentiate between combatants and civilians, which helps guerrilla fighters to blend in with the local population and maintain their anonymity.

The essence of guerrilla warfare is characterized by the hit-and-run tactic, which entails launching sudden and surprise attacks, followed by a swift withdrawal from the battlefield. It is possible for irregular forces to inflict damage on their opponents while simultaneously reducing the risk of direct contact through the utilization of this approach. Over a period of time, the objective is to confuse and wear out the adversary.

Protracted wars: Guerrilla warfare is frequently associated with wars that last for an extended period of time. The objective of irregular forces is not to engage in decisive battles but rather to achieve a sustained campaign of attrition with the objective of wearing down the enemy. With the end goal of attaining political or strategic objectives, the purpose is to weaken the will and resources of the conventional forces.

Guerrilla Warfare Campaigns That Had a Significant Impact:

Viet Cong in the Vietnam War: During the Vietnam War, the Viet Cong, which was the guerrilla arm of the National Liberation Front, used guerilla tactics against the United States military, which was technologically superior. The deep jungles of Vietnam provided the perfect terrain for carrying out ambushes, hit-and-run attacks, and tunnel networks that were designed to impede the progress of regular forces.

Defense of Afghan Mujahideen Against the Soviet Union During the Soviet-Afghan War, which lasted from 1979 to 1989, the Afghan Mujahideen employed guerilla tactics in order to fight back against the Soviet occupation. There were a number of factors that contributed to the lengthy character of the fight, including the rough terrain of Afghanistan, the experience of the Mujahideen in the region, and the support they received from the local communities.

Che Guevara and the Cuban Revolution: Che Guevara, a significant player in the Cuban Revolution, was instrumental in utilizing guerrilla tactics against the Batista regime. He played a major part in this. Guevara's emphasis on organizing the peasantry and carrying out hit-and-run operations in the Sierra Maestra mountains were two of the most important factors that contributed considerably to the eventual triumph of the revolution.

The contemporary dynamics of global insurgencies and their implications:

Insurgencies in the Middle East: Guerrilla warfare has emerged as a key characteristic of wars in the Middle East over the course of the last few decades. Many insurgent groups, including the Taliban in Afghanistan and other factions in Iraq and Syria, have used hit-and-run strategies, suicide bombers, and asymmetrical warfare against conventional military forces. These tactics have been used against conventional military forces.

Warfare methods Employed by Terrorist Organizations Guerrilla techniques have been included into the methods employed by terrorist organizations that engage in hybrid warfare. Hezbollah in Lebanon is one example of a group that has mixed unconventional military tactics with conventional military assets, which has presented obstacles to the conventional military responses.

The progression of technology has had an effect on the dynamics of guerilla warfare. guerilla warfare has been influenced by technological advancements. Social media platforms are now being utilized by irregular forces for the purposes of recruitment, propaganda, and communication. Furthermore, developments in armament and monitoring technologies present guerrilla fighters and their foes with a number of obstacles as well as opportunities.

Urban Guerrilla Warfare: The characteristics of guerrilla warfare have been altered as a result of the trend toward urbanization. The Islamic State in Mosul and the Tamil Tigers in Sri Lanka are two examples of insurgent groups that operate in urban environments. These groups have changed their strategies in order to take advantage of the complexity that come with living in densely populated places.

The Obstacles and Potential Solutions:

Strategies of Counterinsurgency Conventional military forces that are confronted with guerrilla warfare frequently deploy counterinsurgency (COIN) strategies. COIN is a strategy that combines military, political, and socio-economic measures with the objective of gaining the support of the local populace, isolating insurgents, and addressing the underlying reasons of the insurgency.

Considerations of an Ethical Nature The unusual nature of guerrilla warfare offers issues of an ethical nature for both conventional militaries and irregular groups. The use of guerrilla tactics, such as blending in with civilian populations, might cause the distinction between fighters and non-combatants to become more difficult to discern, which raises worries about the possibility of civilian casualties and violations of human rights.

Adapting to Hybrid Threats: Modern battles frequently entail hybrid threats, which are characterized by the combination of guerrilla tactics, conventional military capabilities, and cyber warfare. In order to effectively address such complex difficulties, it is necessary for military forces to adapt and combine a wide variety of capabilities, such as intelligence, technological advancements, and diplomatic undertakings.

The Implications of Future Trends and Tendencies:

Cyber Warfare and Information Operations: The incorporation of cyberwarfare and information operations into guerrilla tactics is anticipated to have a significant impact on the evolution of future conflicts. Through the utilization of cyber capabilities, non-state actors have the potential to disrupt infrastructure, carry out propaganda campaigns, and exert influence over public opinion on a worldwide scale.

The development of autonomous weaponry and robots has the potential to disrupt the dynamics of guerilla warfare. This is because of the possible influence that these technologies could have. The use of drones, for instance, presents a number of issues and ethical questions in relation to civilian casualties, despite the fact that they could be advantageous in terms of monitoring and targeted strikes.

Considerations Regarding the Environment The effects of climate change and the degradation of the environment may have an effect on the dynamics of guerilla warfare. Scarcity of resources, rivalry for water and arable land, and displacement as a result of environmental causes are all potential variables that could perhaps contribute to the creation of new conflicts that include aspects of guerrilla warfare.

Guerrilla warfare, which has its origins that can be traced back through the annals of history, remains a strategy that is both active and influential in the wars that are taking place today. At every stage of history, from ancient battlefields to contemporary urban centers, irregular forces have proved the tenacity and adaptability of guerrilla tactics when confronted with foes that possess superior technological capabilities.

The legacy of guerilla warfare continues to be profoundly ingrained in the strategic landscape, despite the fact that the nature of combat is changing as a result of technological breakthroughs, shifts in global geopolitics, and environmental issues. It is necessary for military strategists, policymakers, and academics who are looking for effective responses to the multifarious challenges that are provided by unconventional conflicts to have a comprehensive understanding of the complexity of irregular warfare.

The persistent legacy of guerilla warfare highlights the significance of addressing not only the military components of conflicts but also the sociopolitical, economic, and ethical facets of these conflicts. The lessons that can be learned from the historical tapestry of guerrilla warfare give essential insights that may be used to shape more effective and ethical responses in a global landscape that is always changing. This is especially important as the globe navigates an era that is characterized by hybrid threats and unconventional techniques.

4.1 Effectiveness of guerrilla tactics

In a variety of conflicts, both historical and contemporary, guerrilla tactics have shown to be extremely effective. These tactics are characterized by their unorthodox nature and their dependence on mobility, surprise, and support from the local community. This article investigates the elements that contribute to the effectiveness of guerrilla tactics. It does so by analyzing case studies from various time periods in order to show the impact that guerrilla tactics have on the outcomes of military operations and the challenges that they present to conventional forces.

Capacity for Adaptation and Exploitation of Terrain:

Flexibility and Adaptability: The ability of guerrilla tactics to be flexible and adaptable is one of the most significant advantages employed by these strategies. The ability to immediately modify their methods in reaction to shifting conditions is a characteristic of guerrilla forces, which are often structured in small, decentralized units. Because they are able to adapt, they are able to take advantage of weaknesses in the enemy's strategy and respond to threats that are always evolving.

Exploitation of Terrain: Guerrilla warfare frequently takes place in terrains that are difficult and complicated, and conventional troops may have difficulty maintaining control of these terrains. There are irregular forces that make use of their understanding of the local topography to their advantage, making use of natural characteristics such as mountains, jungles, or urban areas. The utilization of this terrain offers options for ambush, concealment, and escape routes.

Hit-and-run strategies and asymmetrical behavior:

Asymmetrical combat: Guerrilla tactics are particularly effective in asymmetrical combat, which is characterized by conventional military forces having enhanced firepower and technological capabilities. As a result of the asymmetry, irregular forces are able to avoid direct encounters and instead concentrate on distracting the enemy through the use of hit-and-run strategies. The hazards that are involved with confronting a more powerful foe head-on are reduced for guerrilla fighters since they avoid engaging in pitched conflicts.

Hit-and-Run Tactics: The hit-and-run characteristic of guerrilla warfare comprises surprise strikes followed by a fast retreat, which prevents the opponent from effectively responding to the attack. The conventional troops' morale and resources are depleted as a result of this ongoing harassment, which results in a confrontation that is drawn out and emotionally demanding for everybody involved.

Support from the Community and Insurgency:

Embedded inside Communities: Guerrilla forces frequently embed themselves within local communities, obtaining the support of the public, which is essential to their success. Through this support, the irregular forces receive intelligence, recruits, and assistance with their logistical needs. Conventional troops have a difficult time distinguishing between combatants and non-combatants due to the intimate contact they have with civilians.

The formation of insurgent networks within communities provides guerrilla forces with the opportunity to collect intelligence, disseminate propaganda, and recruit individuals who are sympathetic to their cause. The effectiveness of conventional military techniques is diminished as a result of this network-centric approach, which improves their ability to conduct covert operations.

Impact on the Political and Psychological System:

Guerrilla warfare is not only about participation in military battles; rather, it is frequently linked with the pursuit of political goals. Irregular troops have the objective of weakening the political will of their opponents as well as the determination of their own communities. The use of guerilla tactics, which involve avoiding decisive confrontations, makes the war more about endurance and attrition, with the intention of altering the outcomes of political conflicts.

Warfare from a Psychological Perspective Guerrilla tactics make use of psychological warfare in order to induce fear, confusion, and doubt in the minds of both enemy soldiers and civilian populations. An environment of uneasiness is created as a result of the persistent danger of ambushes, sabotage, and guerrilla attacks, which has an effect on the mental resilience of conventional forces.

Guerrilla tactics in the 21st century

Insurgencies in the Middle East: Guerrilla tactics continue to be highly effective against conventional military forces in contemporary conflicts such as those that are taking place in Iraq, Afghanistan, and Syria. Hit-and-run attacks, suicide bombings, and other insurgency techniques are utilized by insurgent groups, such as the Taliban and numerous factions in the Middle East, in order to fight against foreign occupiers.

Urban Guerrilla Tactics and Hybrid Warfare: The incorporation of guerrilla tactics into hybrid warfare has become a defining characteristic of contemporary wars. For the purpose of capitalizing on the difficulties of densely inhabited places, insurgent groups that operate in urban environments, such as the Islamic State of Iraq and Syria (ISIS) in Mosul, modify their strategy. Urban guerrilla tactics present conventional troops with a unique set of obstacles, which necessitates the development of novel countermeasures.

Conventional forces face a number of challenges, and counterinsurgency strategies are among them

Counterinsurgency (COIN) methods: When confronted with guerrilla warfare, conventional military forces frequently utilize counterinsurgency (COIN) methods. A comprehensive strategy that integrates military, political, and socio-economic measures is necessary for the implementation of COIN. Important aspects of counterintelligence operations include gaining the support of the local populace, isolating militants, and addressing the underlying reasons of the conflict.

Ethical Considerations The efficacy of guerrilla tactics frequently creates ethical concerns for both conventional and irregular formations of the armed forces. The adoption of measures such as blending in with civilian populations might result in an increase in the number of civilian casualties, which raises problems regarding the morality of particular guerrilla strategies and the response of conventional forces.

Understanding the Implications of Future Trends and Adapting to the Challenges of the 21st Century

Cyber Warfare and Information Operations: The incorporation of cyber-warfare and information operations into guerrilla tactics is anticipated to have a significant impact on the evolution of future conflicts. It is possible for non-state actors to use cyber capabilities for disruptive goals, such as influencing public opinion and executing propaganda campaigns on a worldwide scale.

Considerations Regarding the Environment The effects of climate change and the degradation of the environment may have an effect on the dynamics of guerilla warfare. Scarcity of resources, rivalry for water and arable land, and displacement as a result of environmental causes are all potential variables that could perhaps contribute to the creation of new conflicts that include aspects of guerrilla warfare.

Guerrilla tactics, which originated in the annals of history and have since been adapted to the complexity of modern combat, continue to be extremely effective, particularly when it comes to opposing conventional military forces. They are a robust and long-lasting approach because of the variables that contribute to their effectiveness, which include adaptability, asymmetry, local support, and political impact.

The lessons that can be learnt from historical and present instances of guerilla warfare provide vital insights at a time when the world is struggling to understand the ever-changing security issues that it faces. Military strategists, policymakers, and academics have a responsibility to acknowledge the adaptability and dynamism of irregular forces. They must also develop plans that not only address military responses but also address the sociopolitical, economic, and ethical components of war.

The efficacy of guerrilla tactics highlights the necessity of adopting broad and nuanced approaches to security that go beyond the paradigms of standard military operations. The continuing legacy of irregular warfare serves as a reminder that, in a global context that is always shifting, it is necessary to comprehend and respond to the dynamics of guerrilla tactics in order to successfully navigate the intricacies of modern combat.

4.2 Notable instances of successful guerrilla resistance

Throughout the course of history, guerrilla resistance, which is characterized by unusual strategies, tenacity, and the capacity to modify tactics strategically, has been an essential factor in determining the outcomes of a great number of battles. The purpose of this essay is to investigate prominent cases of effective guerrilla resistance, with the goal of analyzing the important aspects that contributed to their victories and the lessons that they give going forward.

Viet Cong participation in the Vietnam War:

The Viet Cong's guerila fight against the United States during the Vietnam War is widely regarded as one of the most famous examples of irregular warfare. This resistance was aided by the terrain advantage and the support of the local population. Viet Cong forces were able to make effective use of the difficult terrain in Vietnam, where they were operating in the vast jungles of the country. Their in-depth familiarity with the surrounding terrain, in conjunction with the enormous support they received from rural areas, enabled them to develop an efficient network that was able to confound the technologically advanced United States military systems.

Tunnel Systems and Hit-and-Run Tactics: The Viet Cong's expertise of hit-and-run tactics proved to be extremely effective with their tunnel systems. It was difficult for conventional troops to engage in protracted action because of the presence of small, mobile formations that assaulted United States forces and then rapidly vanished into the deep forest. As a result of the massive tunnel systems, the Viet Cong were able to maintain their resistance despite the overwhelming firepower of their foes. These tunnel systems provided refuge, hiding places, and communication lines.

The guerrilla struggle of the Viet Cong was not only a military strategy; rather, it was strongly intertwined with political goals. This made the Viet Cong's morale and political endurance extremely important. The political will of the United States of America and its allies was weakened as a result of the prolonged length of the struggle. The determination and tenacity of the Viet Cong, in conjunction with the widespread anti-war sentiments that prevailed around the world, played a role in the final reunification of Vietnam and the withdrawal of United States forces from the country.

Mujahideen of Afghanistan in Opposition to the Soviet Union:

The Afghan Mujahideen's successful guerrilla fight against the Soviet Union throughout the 1980s demonstrated the effects of irregular warfare in a terrain that was both difficult and diverse. This was accomplished through the utilization of local knowledge. Afghanistan's hilly terrain offered inherent benefits for guerrilla tactics, which were utilized by the Afghan government. Because of their familiarity with the area, the Mujahideen were able to effectively confront Soviet soldiers and put up a fight against occupation.

External Support and International Solidarity: The Afghan Mujahideen were provided with a substantial amount of support from external parties, such as the United States of America, Pakistan, and Saudi Arabia. By giving them essential resources, training, and armament, this international solidarity helped to enhance their efforts and provide them with a boost. In their fight against a great super-power, the Mujahideen were able to maintain their resilience thanks to the mix of local knowledge and help from outside sources.

The Mujahideen's ability to adjust their strategies and build a loose but effective coalition against the Soviet Union exemplified the significance of factional unity due to the fact that it demonstrated the Mujahideen's capacity to adapt their tactics accordingly. Despite the fact that they were ideologically and ethnically distinct from one another, numerous Afghan resistance groups came together to fight against the same adversary. Ultimately, the Soviet Union's exit from Afghanistan was one of the factors that contributed to this flexibility and togetherness.

The Cuban Revolution and Che Guevara:

Through his participation in the Cuban Revolution, Che Guevara was able to demonstrate the efficacy of guerrilla tactics in the context of a rural insurgency. Peasant mobilization was also a significant factor in this. Both Guevara and Fidel Castro were responsible for leading a small group of insurgents in the Sierra Maestra highlands. They were responsible for organizing peasants and carrying out hit-and-run operations. The revolutionaries were able to gradually increase their influence and acquire support from the local community by concentrating their efforts on rural areas.

One of the most influential factors in the Cuban Revolution was Che Guevara's charismatic and symbolic leadership, which also played a significant role in the dissemination of propaganda. Through the skillful utilization of his image, beliefs, and revolutionary fervor in propaganda efforts, he was able to inspire not only Cubans but also individuals from all across Latin America and beyond. There was a significant contribution to the success of the revolution made by the combination of military strategy and symbolic leadership.

Long-Term Vision and Strategic Patience: The Cuban Revolution is a prime example of the significance of employing strategic patience and maintaining a long-term perspective when engaging in guerilla resistance. In spite of early failures and difficulties, the revolutionaries led by Fidel Castro and Che Guevara persisted, gradually building support and momentum over the course of several years. Their dedication to a revolutionary cause and their unmistakable vision for a Cuba that has been transformed were two of the most important factors that contributed to their final triumph.

In Macedonia, the National Liberation Army (NLA) is responsible for:

Capacity for Adaptation: The National Liberation Army (NLA) in Macedonia, which was active in the early 2000s, served as an example of the adaptability of guerrilla forces in the modern period. In order to defeat Macedonian government forces, the National Liberation Army (NLA), which was composed of ethnic Albanians, employed hit-and-run strategies, ambushes, and guerilla warfare. The dynamic nature of guerrilla resistance was mirrored in their capacity to adapt to the geopolitical situation and capitalize on ethnic conflicts.

Mobilization of Ethnic Groups and External Factors: The National Liberation Army (NLA) was able to garner support from the ethnic Albanian community in Macedonia by capitalizing on their grievances and rallying support for their cause. Another aspect that contributed to the continuation of the National Liberation Army's struggle was the assistance it received from diaspora populations and surrounding countries that were sympathetic to the cause. The success of their guerrilla tactics was largely attributable to the fact that they had support from both the local community and from outside sources.

The Lessons Learned and Their Relevance to the Present Day:

Adaptability and Local Dynamics: Across these instances of successful guerrilla resistance, a consistent theme emerges—the adaptability of irregular forces to local dynamics and terrain. For guerrilla tactics to be successful, it is essential to have a thorough understanding of the specific characteristics of the operating environment and to change tactics accordingly.

The integration of political objectives with military strategies is a recurrent issue. Political engagement and popular support are also important. Successful guerrilla movements frequently interact with political reality, contributing to the formation of public opinion and gaining support from the general populace. The persistence and duration of guerrilla resistance can be attributed, in part, to the alignment of military tactics with greater political goals.

International Solidarity and Support from Outside Sources: The effectiveness of guerrilla movements has been significantly influenced by the assistance that has been provided from outside sources. This assistance can take the shape of resources, training, or diplomatic backing. The impact of local resistance is amplified by international solidarity, which also gives key advantages when confronted with more powerful foes from other countries.

Propaganda and Symbolic Leadership: Symbolic leadership, which is exemplified by people such as Che Guevara, plays a role in boosting the morale and motivation of guerrilla forces. In order to affect the outcome of a war, it is possible to make effective use of propaganda in order to not only motivate local supporters but also attract the attention of foreign audiences.

Strategic Patience and Long-Term Vision: Guerrilla resistance is frequently a combat that lasts for a considerable amount of time. Examples of success highlight the significance of having a long-term perspective and being patient with a strategic approach. It is more likely that guerrilla groups will be successful in accomplishing their goals if they are able to persevere through initial difficulties and discouragements while maintaining their dedication to their cause.

The fact that irregular warfare techniques have been successful in the past in opposing conventional forces is evidenced by the history of successful guerrilla resistance. The use of guerilla tactics has left an everlasting impression on the progression of history, whether it be in the jungles of Vietnam, the mountains of Afghanistan, or the rural landscapes of Cuba.

Within the context of the modern geopolitical situation, the lessons that were acquired from these examples of successful resistance continue to be pertinent. The adaptability, political engagement, and strategic patience that are inherent in guerrilla tactics provide useful insights for those who are negotiating the challenges of irregular warfare. This is because conflicts continue to evolve.

The long legacy of guerrilla resistance serves as a reminder that, even in the face of overwhelming odds, irregular forces that are inventive and dedicated have the ability to change the fate of nations and affect the course of events on a global scale. The historical tapestry of guerrilla resistance provides a rich source of learning that may be used to understand and respond to the dynamics of conflict in the 21st century. This is especially relevant as the world is increasingly confronted with new problems.

Chapter 5

Cultural Independence

Independence from one's culture is a fundamental component of human identity. It is the embodiment of the distinctive expressions, customs, and beliefs that set one group or nation apart from another. As a result of globalization and increased interconnection, the maintenance and celebration of cultural autonomy have become of the utmost importance in order to ensure the continuation of a wide range of heritages. The numerous aspects of cultural independence are investigated in this essay. The value of cultural independence, the difficulties associated with it, and the methods in which communities all over the world navigate the intricate relationship between tradition and modernity are all discussed.

Identifying the Core of One's Identity Through the Concept of Cultural Independence

At its root, cultural independence refers to the autonomy and resilience of a community's cultural heritage. There is also a connection between cultural expression and cultural heritage. It covers a diverse array of customs, languages, arts, and traditions that have been handed down from generation to generation with great care and attention. Independence of culture is not only the act of preserving the past in a static manner; rather, it is a dynamic process that enables civilizations to develop while still retaining their fundamental essence.

Language as a Foundational Component: Language frequently functions as a foundational component of cultural autonomy. A community's identity can be strengthened by the maintenance and utilization of a distinct language, which also serves as a medium for the transmission of values, stories, and collective memories throughout the community. In order to preserve cultural diversity, it is essential to make efforts to preserve or restore languages that are in danger of extinction.

The Importance of Maintaining One's Cultural Independence:

Independence from culture is inextricably linked to the maintenance of one's identity, which cannot be separated from cultural autonomy. The act of providing individuals with a sense of belonging and continuity, so connecting them to their roots and establishing a shared understanding of who they are, creates a sense of continuity. Considering the impacts of globalization, which tend to make people more similar to one another, cultural independence emerges as a potent instrument for establishing and maintaining distinctive identities.

On a worldwide scale, cultural independence is an asset that contributes to the mosaic of human civilization. Globally, cultural diversity is an asset. By providing a variety of viewpoints, artistic manifestations, and approaches to comprehending the world, the richness of our collective history is enhanced by the diversity of cultural expressions. To cultivate a worldwide environment that celebrates diversity rather than conformity, it is necessary to acknowledge and respect the independence of cultural practices.

Resilience in the Face of Change: Communities that are confronted with external pressures and socio-economic shifts might find a source of resilience in their cultural independence. It is possible for communities to manage obstacles without surrendering their identity if they have the ability to adapt while maintaining fundamental cultural aspects during the process. The manner in which civilizations have persisted and developed over the course of millennia are evidence of this resilience.

Obstacles to the Acquiring of Cultural Independence:

Globalization and the homogenization of cultures: The rapid spread of globalized influences, which is made possible by technology and communication, presents a fundamental challenge to the concept of cultural autonomy. A dominating global culture can be the driving force behind cultural homogenization, which can result in the erosion of distinctive traditions, languages, and ways of life, ultimately leading to a loss of variety.

Changes in lifestyle, attitudes, and societal structures are frequently brought about by the process of modernization. Traditional practices are also subject to these changes. There are some aspects of modernization that can be adopted without losing cultural independence; but, there is a risk that old behaviors, particularly those that are regarded incompatible with current values, may face marginalization or even extinction.

Appropriation and Exploitation of Culture Communities may also have to contend with circumstances in which elements of their culture are appropriated or exploited by other forces for the purpose of achieving financial or superficial goals. It is possible that the authenticity and value of traditions could be diminished as a result of cultural appropriation, which presents problems around respect, permission, and the commercialization of traditions.

The Independence of Indigenous Communities with Regard to Their Cultures:

The bond that indigenous tribes have with the land is inextricably connected to their cultural autonomy, and this connection is essential to the preservation of their integrity. As a result of the fact that the land contains sacred sites, ancestral ties, and the resources that are necessary for traditional practices, the preservation of traditional territory is frequently at the center of the process of preserving cultural integrity.

The legacy of colonialism and the resurgence of indigenous cultures Numerous indigenous populations have been subjected to historical injustices, such as the repression of their culture and the forced assimilation that ensued under colonial control. Currently, there is a resurgence of initiatives to reclaim and rehabilitate indigenous languages, arts, and rituals. These efforts are being revived in contemporary times. Independence from one's culture becomes an essential component in the process of reclaiming one's identity and recovering from the traumas of the past.

Stewardship of the Environment: In indigenous contexts, cultural autonomy frequently encompasses actions related to environmental stewardship. Several indigenous societies have activities that are environmentally friendly deeply ingrained in their respective traditions. The maintenance of cultural autonomy requires not only the protection of cultural activities but also the preservation of the ecosystems that are connected with those practices.

Supporting the Independence of Cultural Practices:

Education and Awareness: Education is one of the most important factors in fostering both cultural independence and awareness. The incorporation of a wide range of cultural perspectives into educational programs helps students develop an appreciation and appreciation for the various ways of life. An respect for the richness of human diversity can be fostered through the implementation of cultural awareness initiatives, which contribute to the dismantling of stereotypes.

Cultural Revitalization Initiatives: Initiatives that strive to revitalize cultural practices, languages, and arts contribute to the maintenance of cultural independence if they are successful. Participation in language immersion programs, cultural festivals, and projects that document and pass on traditional knowledge to future generations are examples of what can fall under this category.

Legislation and Policy Support: Governments and international entities have the potential to play a significant role in promoting cultural independence by enacting legislation and policies that safeguard indigenous rights, encourage linguistic diversity, and address concerns over cultural appropriation. It is of the utmost importance to acknowledge and respect the fact that communities have the ability to determine their own cultural agendas.

The role of globalization: Does it bridge cultural divides or does it erode cultural autonomy?

Hybrid Identities and Cultural interaction Globalization, despite the fact that it poses problems to cultural autonomy, also makes it easier for people to engage in cultural interaction and gives rise to hybrid identities.

Because of the interconnected nature of the modern world, it is possible to exchange cultural expressions, which in turn helps to cultivate a global discourse that has the potential to enrich rather than erode cultural diversity.

Digital Connectivity and Cultural Expression: The ability of communities to share their cultural expressions with a worldwide audience is made possible by digital platforms, which present opportunities that have never been seen before. Digital connectedness enables communities to assert their cultural independence, challenge stereotypes, and make connections with individuals all over the world who share similar values and perspectives. This is true for anything from social media to the development of material online.

Independence of Culture in the Production of Art:

Literature and Language Preservation: Literature emerges as a potent instrument for the preservation and promotion of cultural and linguistic autonomy. Authors who write in their mother tongues not only contribute to the preservation of language but also offer distinctive viewpoints that question the mainstream narratives surrounding the subject. Literature acts as a conduit for communication between different civilizations and a window into a variety of worldviews.

There is a connection between the visual arts and the process of identity development. The visual arts, which include painting, sculpture, and other kinds of artistic expression, are important components of this process. For the purpose of conveying messages of resiliency, resistance, and celebration, artists frequently draw inspiration from cultural symbols, motifs, and traditions. Art emerges as a vehicle that facilitates the assertion and dissemination of cultural autonomy around the world.

A worldwide language that is not limited by borders, music acts as a medium through which cultural narratives can be discussed. The preservation and invention of historic musical forms, the investigation of current genres that are anchored in cultural narratives, and the global distribution of distinctive sounds that represent a variety of identities are all aspects of cultural independence in the realm of music.

Achieving a Balance Between Tradition and Progress in the Modern Era: Challenges in the Modern Era

Changes in Generations and the Transmission of Culture The generational transition presents obstacles to cultural independence because younger members of a community may accept features of modernity that are different from traditional behaviors. In order to maintain cultural continuity, it is necessary to strike a balance between the transmission of cultural knowledge from one generation to the next while also allowing for the development of manifestations.

Cultural Displacement and Urbanization: As populations move to metropolitan areas in search of economic opportunity, urbanization frequently results in the displacement of their cultural traditions. The transition from rural to urban contexts can have an effect on more traditional ways of life, languages, and traditions, which can create obstacles for the preservation of cultural autonomy.

Cultural Openness and Inclusivity: As societies grow increasingly interconnected, promoting cultural independence entails managing the delicate balance between conserving distinct identities and developing cultural openness. This is a challenge that must be overcome in order to achieve cultural independence. In the midst of a wide variety of cultural manifestations, inclusivity becomes particularly important because it paves the way for discourse, mutual respect, and the celebration of shared humanity.

In a future that is increasingly globalized, Cultural Independence:

Innovations in Technology and the Exchange of Cultures It is highly probable that future technology developments will further affect the terrain of cultural autonomy. There is a possibility that breakthroughs such as virtual reality, augmented reality, and others could provide new opportunities for immersive cultural encounters, which will in turn foster a greater understanding and appreciation of a variety of traditions.

Local Autonomy and Global Citizenship: Finding a middle ground between global citizenship and local autonomy will be a defining challenge in the future. An approach that is nuanced and inclusive is required in order to foster a sense of shared humanity while simultaneously respecting the liberty of communities to determine the course of their cultural destinies in a world that is undergoing fast change.

The fabric of human civilization is built on the foundation of cultural autonomy, which is characterized by the complex interaction between modernity and tradition. At a time when the globe is struggling to negotiate the difficulties of a globalized era, the necessity of preserving, celebrating, and respecting the various cultural expressions that exist is becoming increasingly urgent.

It is imperative that the concepts of equality, justice, and inclusivity serve as the foundation for projects that aim to foster cultural independence. The recognition of the intrinsic importance of every culture, language, and tradition not only helps to preserve the distinct identities of individuals, but it also contributes to the construction of a global tapestry that reflects the richness and diversity of the human experience.

Through the process of cultivating cultural autonomy, communities go on a journey of self-discovery, resiliency, and mutual comprehension. The future holds the promise of a society in which cultural diversity is not only preserved but is embraced as a source of power, togetherness, and collective wisdom for generations to come. This has the potential to manifest itself in the future.

5.1 Analysis of Afghan cultural values

Afghanistan, a country with a long and illustrious history and a diverse ethnic tapestry, is a country in which cultural values play a significant part in the formation of daily life, social relationships, and the larger social fabric. In order to have a complete understanding of Afghan cultural values, it is necessary to conduct a detailed investigation of the customs, conventions, and belief systems that have persisted over the course of centuries. Additionally, it is necessary to acknowledge the impact of external influences and the difficulties that are brought about by modernization. In order to present an examination of Afghan cultural values, the purpose of this essay is to delve into essential components that characterize the social and ethical environment of the Afghan people.

The Importance of Islam as a Foundational Component of Afghan Identity

The influence of Islam on Afghan culture Islam occupies a major role in Afghan cultural values, and it exerts an influence on a variety of areas of daily life, governance, and social relations. There is a sizable minority of Afghans who embrace Shia Islam, while the majority of Afghans adhere to Sunni Islam. As a result of the tight connection that is created between religion and culture, ethical considerations, social conventions, and the legal system are all guided by Islamic principles.

Islamic Rituals and Traditions in Everyday Life The Islamic rituals and traditions are strongly ingrained in the daily life of women in Afghanistan. Observances such as the daily prayers, the fasting that occurs during the month of Ramadan, and the celebration of Islamic holidays such as Eid al-Fitr and Eid al-Adha are fundamental to the culture of Afghanistan. In addition, the influence of Islam may be seen in the many types of family structures, gender roles, and the dynamics of the community.

The importance of family and community in Afghan society

Individualism and Extended Families: The values of Afghan culture place a strong emphasis on the concept of collectivism and the significance of extended family networks. The idea of "hamisha," which can be translated as "extended family," encompasses a wider network of relatives beyond the traditional nuclear family in which individuals are raised. The sense of belonging, social support, and financial help that are all provided by this interconnection are all benefits.

Traditional gender roles are highly engrained in Afghan society, and there are unique expectations for men and women alike. Family honor is also a significant aspect of Afghan culture. Despite the fact that males frequently take on positions such as decision-makers and breadwinners, women have traditionally been responsible for managing the household and maintaining the relationships within the family. The honor of the family is of the utmost importance, and the upholding of society norms is inextricably linked to the preservation of the family's reputation.

Hospitality and the Customs of Social Interaction:

Pashtunwali Code: The Pashtunwali Code, which is the customary code of the Pashtun people, has a great impact on the cultural values that are held in Afghanistan. It includes values such as melmastia, which means hospitality, nanawatai, which means justice, and namus, which means honor, which means to safeguard one's honor. Through the use of Pashtunwali, social interactions, the resolution of disagreements, and the preservation of a sense of honor within the community are all guided.

Culture of Tea and Socialization: The Afghan practice of providing tea to guests is a way of expressing hospitality to visitors. Warmth, welcome, and a dedication to the development of relationships are all conveyed via the act of sharing tea. The activity of socializing over tea is rather prevalent, and it affords people of the community the opportunity to get together, exchange stories, and improve their social links among themselves.

The preservation of cultural heritage through the use of language and oral tradition

Although Dari and Pashto are the official languages of Afghanistan, the linguistic landscape of Afghanistan is distinguished by diversity. Dari and Pashto are the two languages that serve as the official languages. In order to reflect the historical and ethnic diversity of Afghanistan, the preservation of these languages is an essential component of the country's cultural values. While Pashto is the primary language in areas where Pashtuns make up the majority of the population, Dari, a variety of Persian, is spoken in urban centers.

Oral Tradition and Storytelling: The oral tradition is extremely important to Afghan culture and occupies a distinguished position. In order to contribute to the transfer of cultural values from one generation to the next, elders are responsible for the oral transmission of stories, myths, and historical narratives. Storytelling is not only a method of preserving tradition, but it is also a method of passing on social lessons and cultural knowledge to future generations.

How to Strike a Balance Between Tradition and Progress in Education and Modernization

Despite the fact that traditional cultural norms lay a strong focus on the significance of education, there are still many obstacles to overcome within the realm of educational attainment, particularly in rural areas. The achievement of an education might be hampered by a variety of factors, including gender inequality, worries around security, and poor infrastructure. It is a difficult job to strike a balance between the necessity for modern education and the preservation of historically significant values.

Growing up in a digital age, the younger generation in Afghanistan is navigating the junction of traditional cultural norms and global influences. This is a challenge that they face because they are growing up in a digital age. The utilization of technology, the exposure to international media, and the availability of information all present opportunities and problems for the purpose of forming the viewpoints of young people in Afghanistan.

Craftsmanship and the Arts: Expressions of Individuality and Identity

Artistic Expressions of Culture: Rugs & Carpets

Rugs and carpets from Afghanistan are recognized all over the world for their unique designs and skilled craftsmanship. The technique of carpet weaving is profoundly established in Afghan culture, and each rug frequently tells a tale through the patterns and symbolism that it contains. This time-honored craft not only provides a means of subsistence for a great number of Afghan households, but it also makes a significant contribution to the cultural identity of the country.

Calligraphy and Islamic Art: Calligraphy is a significant part of Afghan artistic expression, and it is frequently one of the most important elements in Islamic art. The lines and poetry of the Quran are portrayed with great dexterity, resulting in the creation of visual representations of cultural and spiritual qualities. It is a monument to the artistic richness of Afghan art that calligraphy, geometric designs, and brilliant colors all connect with one another throughout the work.

Festivals and celebrations are celebrations of joy that are culturally significant

Known as Nowruz, the celebration of the New Year, Nowruz, also known as the Afghan New Year, is an important cultural event that commemorates the beginning of spring. Joy, rebirth, and the coming together of the community are all hallmarks of this season. The cultural significance of Nowruz is shown in the fact that families meet together to celebrate the holiday by eating together, exchanging gifts, and participating in other festive activities.

Celebrations of Eid: Islamic Festivals Both Eid al-Fitr and Eid al-Adha are significant Islamic holidays that are celebrated with a great deal of excitement in Afghanistan. At these events, communal prayers, feasts, and acts of charity are performed, with the purpose of highlighting the virtues of compassion, generosity, and communal solidarity that are deeply ingrained in the cultural traditions of Afghanistan.

The Cultural Responses to Adversity of Conflict and Resilience

Afghanistan's history has been marked by periods of conflict and foreign invasions, but the country has managed to remain resilient throughout these times. Throughout all of these difficulties, the cultural values of Afghanistan, which are based on resiliency and togetherness, have been an essential factor in assisting communities in enduring hardship. One of the factors that has contributed to the Afghan people's resilience is their capacity to take strength from their cultural identity.

Preservation of Cultural legacy: Afghanistan's cultural legacy has been threatened by conflict on multiple occasions. The difficulties that are encountered in the process of maintaining historical places are brought to light by instances of cultural devastation, such as the Buddhas of Bamiyan. When it comes to ensuring that Afghan cultural values are preserved over time, it is absolutely necessary to make efforts to protect cultural items and to support heritage preservation.

Upon conducting an analysis of the cultural values of Afghanistan, it becomes abundantly clear that the beautiful tapestry of Afghanistan is woven with threads of tradition, resiliency, and a profound connection to Islamic ideals. To successfully navigate the complexity of a world that is always changing while also maintaining the core of one's cultural identity is a struggle.

In light of Afghanistan's development toward modernity and global interconnectedness, the delicate equilibrium that exists between tradition and progress is becoming an increasingly important factor to take into consideration. The resiliency that is ingrained in Afghan cultural values, which have been developed by centuries of history, gives a basis for understanding how to navigate the possibilities and difficulties that are still to come.

The preservation of Afghan cultural values is contingent on a concerted effort to celebrate diversity, protect traditions, and cultivate an atmosphere in which the ageless wisdom of Afghan culture can coexist with the dynamism of the modern day. This is to be accomplished in the face of both external influences and internal transformations. As Afghanistan's cultural identity continues to develop, it is durable and firmly embedded in the hearts of its people. This delicate dance between tradition and change is what makes Afghanistan its cultural identity.

5.2 How cultural identity fuels resistance against foreign dominance

Cultural identity, which may be defined as the collective sense of belonging and shared values that characterize a community or nation, emerges as a powerful force when confronted with the dominance of people from other countries. Throughout the course of human history, communities have utilized their cultural identity as a means of bolstering their resilience and resistance against external forces that aim to exert dominance. The purpose of this essay is to investigate the complex dynamics that enable cultural identity to become a rallying point, generating a spirit of defiance and togetherness in the fight against alien rule.

The Role of Cultural Identity in the Resistance Movement:

Definition of Cultural Identity Cultural identity is a complex web of traditions, language, beliefs, and behaviors that contribute to the formation of a community's distinctive personality. The purpose of it is to act as a mirror, reflecting the collective soul of a nation, and to provide a shared story that brings individuals together. As a sign of resistance against attempts to degrade or alter the fundamental nature of a community, the preservation of cultural identity becomes a rallying cry when a community is confronted with the domination of individuals from other countries.

Maintaining Autonomy and Integrity: The autonomy and integrity of a community are inextricably linked to the cultural character of that community. A common aspect of foreign dominance is the attempt to impose external ideals, languages, or systems on a community, which poses a danger to the very foundation of that community's identity. By standing up to such control, communities are able to affirm their right to preserve their own cultural manifestations, ensuring that their history will be preserved for future generations.

The Role of Cultural Identity in the Development of Resilience:

The historical resilience of communities in the face of colonialism: During the whole period of colonialism, communities were subjected to the imposition of foreign rule, economic exploitation, and cultural assimilation. It was in response to this that cultural identity formed as a force that was durable, allowing communities to withstand demands from the outside. Acts of resistance against attempts to subdue and homogenize different cultures were the continuation of languages, traditions, and social systems that had been passed down through generations.

Images of Resistance and Symbols of Culture: Symbols, rituals, and imagery that represent resistance are frequently used as a means of expressing cultural identity. Flags, national anthems, and traditional apparel all become potent symbols of defiance, instilling a sense of pride and unity in the people who wear them. Not only do these cultural markers function as concrete manifestations of identity, but they also serve as focal places for activities that are part of resistance movements.

The Role of Language as a Combat Space:

Language is a fundamental component of cultural identity because it acts as a medium through which values, narratives, and the collective memory of a group can be transmitted. The language of a community is met with vehement opposition whenever there is an attempt to restrict or replace it. As communities fight to retain their linguistic heritage against the dominance of other languages, language becomes a battleground where the struggle for cultural identity is played out.

Campaigns for the Revitalization of Languages: In response to the repression of languages, communities frequently launch language revitalization campaigns. In order to challenge the supremacy of foreign languages that were imposed by colonial or occupying powers, efforts to educate, document, and promote indigenous languages constitute acts of resistance. From this vantage point, language transforms into a tool for the preservation and resistance of cultural traditions.

Resistance and the Identity of Religious Groups:

The importance of religious values as a moral compass many communities place a significant emphasis on religious identity as a component of their cultural identity. Religious ideals that are held in common can frequently act as a moral compass, directing individuals and groups in the acts and relationships they engage in. During periods of foreign rule, religious identity emerges as a form of ethical resistance, exerting an influence not just on individual actions but also on collective and collective activities.

Religion-Based Movements Against Oppression: The annals of history are filled with examples of faith-based movements that have organized themselves to fight against oppression from other countries. Religious identity has been a driving force behind movements that seek justice, autonomy, and the preservation of cultural traditions that are built in faith. These movements have been fueled by anti-colonial efforts as well as resistance against occupying troops.

As a form of defiance, cultural practices are as follows:

Works of Art, Music, and Literature: Cultural practices, such as works of art, music, and literature, become potent mediums of resistance. These messages of defiance, perseverance, and hope are communicated by artists and makers by drawing inspiration from cultural traditions. Creative expressions serve as a counter-narrative to the domination of foreign cultures, bolstering the depth of cultural identity and posing a challenge to efforts to impose other narratives.

Festivals and Celebrations: When it comes to resistance, cultural festivals and celebrations take on a greater significance than they would otherwise. In addition to serving as manifestations of cultural continuity, these events also serve to assert the vitality and longevity of a community's collective identity. Cultural activities, whether they take the form of traditional dances, rituals, or communal gatherings, become acts of defiance against attempts by outsiders to eradicate or suppress indigenous traditions.

Cultural solidarity as a means of achieving unity:

Community Cohesion and Solidarity: A sense of community cohesion and solidarity can be fostered through the cultivation of multicultural identity. Whenever humans are confronted with dangers from the outside world, they draw strength from the cultural heritage that they share. Resistance movements are built on the foundation of the relationships that are formed through the use of a shared language, traditions, and values. These bonds unite different sectors of a community in opposition to the rule of foreign powers.

In the context of resistance, inclusivity and diversity are both important concepts. Cultural identity, while serving as a unifying factor, also embraces difference within a community. Those resistance movements that are motivated by cultural identification frequently demonstrate inclusivity, as they bring together people from a variety of backgrounds who share a dedication to preserving their cultural heritage. The durability of the resistance is strengthened as a result of this diversity, which results in the creation of a mosaic of voices that jointly argue against the supremacy of foreign powers.

Attempts to Overcome Obstacles to Cultural Resistance:

The contemporary era is characterized by globalization, which presents challenges to cultural resistance. Globalization is also associated with cultural erosion. The entry of external influences, media, and economic systems can contribute to the deterioration of culture, which in turn can dilute the values and behaviors that have been practiced traditionally. Those who are fighting against foreign influence need to learn how to navigate the intricacies of a globalized society while yet maintaining their cultural identity.

Internal Divisions and Co-optation: The presence of internal divisions within a community or nation might present difficulties for the process of cultural resistance. There is a possibility that foreign entities will take advantage of internal splits and co-opt aspects of cultural identity for their own purposes. Conquering internal differences becomes absolutely necessary in order to construct a unified front against the supremacy of foreign forces.

Within the ongoing narrative of human history, cultural identity emerges as a guiding light of resistance against the control of foreign powers. In addition to being an act of defiance, the preservation of language, customs, religious values, and artistic expressions becomes a demonstration of the enduring power that communities possess. In the face of efforts to subdue, assimilate, or eradicate the distinctive personality of varied civilizations, cultural identity emerges as a strong adversary due to its capacity to cultivate togetherness, resilience, and a sense of purpose that is shared by all members of the community.

In spite of the fact that the world is constantly struggling with geopolitical transformations, cultural resistance continues to be a crucial component in the process of protecting the richness of human variation. Recognizing and honoring the liberty of communities to determine their own cultural destinies becomes a fundamental component in the process of cultivating a global environment in which varied identities can flourish in harmony. Cultural identity is a monument to the unyielding spirit of communities that are determined to establish their own destinies among the difficulties of a changing world. It stands as a testament in the furnace of resistance.

Chapter 6

Occupation Challenges

The occupation, which is an essential part of the human experience, is confronted with a wide variety of difficulties that have developed throughout the course of history. In the ever-changing environment of the 21st century, individuals are confronted with difficulties in their working lives that have never been seen before. This all-encompassing investigation dives into a variety of dimensions of occupational problems, exploring topics such as technology disruptions, globalization, evolving employment markets, and the socio-psychological aspects of work. We will be better able to negotiate the contemporary occupational landscape, as well as build resilience and flexibility, if we have a greater knowledge of these problems.

The Disruptions Caused by Technology:

Today's workforce faces a number of significant difficulties, one of the most significant being the rapid growth of technology. The introduction of automation, artificial intelligence (AI), and machine learning has brought about a transformation in various industries, which has resulted in the elimination of certain occupations while simultaneously generating other opportunities. Individuals whose skills become obsolete face a significant difficulty as a result of this phenomena, which is frequently referred to as technological unemployment.

A number of traditional manufacturing jobs, administrative positions, and tasks that are routinely performed have been impacted by the rise of automation. It is becoming increasingly difficult for humans to acquire particular talents as computers grow more capable of performing tasks that are repetitive. In order to maintain their relevance in the labor market, workers are required to acquire new skills and improve their existing ones.

The introduction of new technologies, on the other hand, brings about opportunities. The number of available jobs in developing disciplines such as data science, cybersecurity, and the creation of artificial intelligence has increased significantly.

The difficulty lies in cultivating a workforce that is capable of adjusting to the ever-evolving technology world through the process of continual learning and development.

Job Market Dynamics and the Impact of Globalization:

The landscape of employment markets has been drastically altered as a result of globalization, which has been responsible for both obstacles and possibilities.

While it has brought about opportunities for worldwide collaboration and the acquisition of different talent, it has also brought about an increase in the level of competition. Employment opportunities in certain places have been negatively impacted as a result of the widespread practice of outsourcing jobs to nations that have lower prevailing labor prices.

The gig economy, which is defined by work that is performed on a freelance basis and for a shorter period of time, has become increasingly prevalent. Despite the fact that it offers flexibility, it frequently does not give job stability, benefits, or a consistent salary. Many people in today's economy are confronted with the difficulty of finding a way to strike a balance between the advantages of flexibility and the difficulties of job insecurity.

As non-traditional work arrangements continue to gain popularity:

There is no longer a unique paradigm for employment that corresponds to the traditional 9-to-5 workday. The freelance work environment, the gig economy, and working remotely have all become fundamental components of the contemporary labor market. Although these choices provide flexibility, they also come with a number of drawbacks, including the possibility of being isolated, having a blurred line between work and life, and not having a stable career.

During the pandemic that swept the world, many people began accepting remote employment as the norm. This trend was accelerated by technology improvements. Despite the fact that it established that working from any location is possible, it also brought to light a number of obstacles, including digital tiredness, difficulty in communication, and the requirement for comprehensive cybersecurity measures.

The socio-psychological features of these non-traditional work arrangements present a one-of-a-kind set of problems that must be navigated. Innovative ways to leadership and communication are required in order to ensure that a sense of belonging is established and that team cohesion is maintained in a context that is based on gig work or remote work.

Education and the Mismatch Between Skills:

There is frequently a large talent gap as a consequence of the rapid expansion of their respective businesses. There is a possibility that graduates will have skills that are no longer relevant when they enter the workforce since educational systems are having difficulty keeping up with the rapid improvements in technology. Because of this, it is difficult for those looking for work as well as for businesses.

The efforts that are being made to bridge the skill gap, such as vocational training programs, online courses, and cooperation between the industry and academics, are absolutely necessary. However, the difficulty that still needs to be addressed is learning how to adapt education to the continuously shifting requirements of the labor market. Learning that continues throughout one's life has become an absolute requirement, highlighting the significance of having a growth mindset and being able to adapt to fluctuating vocational requirements.

Diversification and inclusion in the workplace:

The achievement of diversity and inclusion in the workplace is a persistent task that has significant repercussions for the success of the organization. In many different fields of endeavor, there is still a persistent problem of underrepresentation of particular demographic groups, such as women, people of color, and people with disabilities.

A multi-pronged strategy is required in order to effectively address this situation. This strategy should include the implementation of proactive diversity hiring practices, the creation of inclusive work cultures, and the promotion of equal chances for career advancement. When it comes to attracting top talent, organizations that promote diversity and inclusion not only have a greater chance of doing so, but they also reap the benefits of a diverse range of perspectives, which in turn drives innovation and creativity.

Mental Health in the Workplace of:

The importance of mental health in the workplace has increased as more and more businesses have been aware of the influence that stress brought on by work may have on the well-being and productivity of their employees. Stress, burnout, and mental health problems are all factors that lead to the blurring of boundaries between work and home life, which, when combined with the pressures of reaching performance standards, contributes to their development.

There is a growing recognition among employers of the significance of mental health support programs, flexible work arrangements, and the promotion of a good work-life balance. On the other hand, resolving issues related to mental health calls for a cultural shift that emphasizes the well-being of employees and eliminates the stigma associated with requesting assistance.

Cultural norms in the workplace and employee participation:

One of the most important factors that determines employee satisfaction, engagement, and retention is the culture that exists within an organization. A toxic work culture, which is characterized by inadequate leadership, a lack of communication, and an environment that is unfriendly, presents a significant problem. A positive culture in the workplace, on the other hand, encourages collaboration, creativity, and a sense of purpose among an employee.

The difficulty of employee engagement, which is a measurement of how focused and devoted individuals are to their work, is one that continues to be ongoing.

There are a number of factors that lead to a more engaged workforce, including clear communication, recognition of achievements, chances for professional development, and a feeling of purpose.

In the 21st century, occupational issues are complex, including technological disruptions, globalization, evolving labor markets, and socio-psychological aspects of work. These obstacles are becoming increasingly difficult to overcome. In order to successfully navigate these problems, a comprehensive approach is required, one that includes human adaptability, organizational flexibility, and organizational support from society.

The ability to accept change, improve one's skills, and cultivate work settings that are inclusive and helpful is becoming increasingly important as we continue to observe the transition that is taking place in the workplace. In the constantly shifting terrain of the modern workforce, individuals and organizations can not only survive but also prosper if they confront these problems head-on and take their responsibilities seriously.

6.1 Logistical hurdles faced by occupying forces

There are other factors than strategic planning and combat effectiveness that contribute to the successful execution of military operations, particularly during occupation. Taking into account logistical factors is one of the most important factors that determines whether or not invading forces will be successful and sustainable. The purpose of this investigation is to investigate the myriad of logistical issues that military forces encounter during occupation. These challenges include the intricacies of supply chains, the difficulties of infrastructure, the cultural considerations, and the requirement for agility in surroundings that are always changing.

Complications in the Supply Chain:

The upkeep of a supply system that is both reliable and effective is of the utmost importance for any occupying force. When it comes to moving personnel, equipment, and supplies to and within the occupied zone, the logistics involved are complex and require careful planning. It is necessary to ensure the safety and upkeep of supply lines, which frequently span extensive distances and have to traverse difficult terrain.

The susceptibility of supply lines to hostile activities, like as ambushes and guerrilla attacks,

adds an additional layer of complication to the situation. Assuring the safety of vital supply lines becomes a continual problem, which calls for the strategic deployment of military assets and resources in order to guarantee that important provisions continue to flow without interruption.

Furthermore, the sheer quantity and variety of supplies that are required by the occupying forces, which include everything from fuel and ammunition to medical resources and food, necessitates effective coordination and timely delivery. The dynamic nature of combat zones, in which conditions can change quickly and have an effect on the accessibility and safety of supply lines, is something that can be challenging for logisticians to take into consideration.

Challenges Facing the Infrastructure:

A great amount of influence is exerted on the logistical capabilities of occupying forces by the state of the infrastructure in the territory that is under occupation. In many instances, military operations are carried out in locations that have infrastructure that is either insufficient or degraded, which creates difficulties for transportation, communication, and overall mobility.

It is possible that roads, bridges, and transportation hubs are damaged or non-existent, which necessitates the expenditure of significant resources for their repair and maintenance. The military forces are required to make investments in the construction of temporary buildings and transportation networks in order to simplify the movement of personnel and supplies. This is because there is a lack of thoroughly established infrastructure.

It is possible that occupying forces will find themselves in regions that have restricted access to fundamental conveniences like clean water and power under certain circumstances. In light of the fact that maintaining military operations and safeguarding the well-being of people are dependent on overcoming such problems, addressing these infrastructure inadequacies becomes a logistical priority.

Considerations Regarding Culture:

Occupying forces frequently act in regions that have cultural norms, traditions, and other societal structures that are distinct from one another. In addition to being essential for diplomatic interactions, it is also essential for logistical purposes to have a solid understanding of and respect for the local culture. The logistics staff is required to manage cultural nuances, which might have an effect on the operations of the supply chain, communication, and collaboration with the populations that are located nearby.

When it comes to overcoming cultural obstacles, some of the most important components are negotiating with local suppliers, maintaining cultural sensitivity in interactions, and adjusting logistics tactics to line with local practices. When this is not done, it can result in skepticism, opposition, and even animosity from the local populace, which further complicates the efforts that are being made to organize logistics.

Capacity for Adaptation in Changeable Environments:

The occupying forces are confronted with the task of operating in surroundings that are both dynamic and unexpected. Because of the fluid nature of combat zones, it is necessary to have a high degree of agility in the planning and execution of logistical operations. When faced with quickly fluctuating circumstances, such as shifting frontlines, developing threat environments, and the introduction of new logistical issues, logisticians are required to adjust their thinking and strategies accordingly.

The capacity to modify supply routes with flexibility, adapt to unanticipated impediments, and respond to emerging threats are all essential components of the ability to adapt to changing circumstances in the logistics industry. Those in charge of occupying territory are required to continually evaluate and reevaluate their logistical techniques in order to guarantee that they continue to be effective in spite of the changing circumstances.

Aspects of the Environment:

The environmental elements that might vary greatly depending on the geography of the land that is occupied add another layer of complexity to the logistical issues that are already there. There is a potential for the efficiency and efficacy of logistical operations to be negatively impacted by harsh weather conditions, excessive temperatures, and hard terrain.

There are specific logistical obstacles that are connected with each location, such as mountainous regions, dense rainforests, and arid desert conditions. Forces that operate in these environments must overcome these challenges. In order to successfully navigate these many situations, it is frequently necessary to have specialized equipment, training, and logistical tactics.

Concerns Relating to Societal Welfare:

Occupying forces are frequently involved in operations that encompass not just military goals but also humanitarian initiatives. These operations are frequently executed. The local populace requires support, medical assistance, and other critical services, all of which require extensive logistical planning in order to be properly delivered. The already difficult logistical picture is made much more difficult by the fact that it is necessary to strike a balance between the requirements of civilian and military organizations.

In order to guarantee that relief is distributed in an effective manner, humanitarian logistics requires coordination among local non-governmental organizations (NGOs), international organizations, and government authorities. Assessing needs, coordinating transportation, and successfully managing regulatory and cultural issues are some of the logistical hurdles that must be overcome in order to provide aid in an efficient manner.

When occupying forces are confronted with a multitude of logistical challenges, these challenges extend beyond the conventional features of military strategy. Collectively, the logistical landscape in occupied regions is shaped by a variety of elements, including the complexity of supply chain operations, the difficulties of infrastructure, cultural concerns, the ability to adapt to dynamic situations, environmental factors, and humanitarian considerations.

A complete and integrated strategy to logistics is required in order to successfully navigate these hurdles. This approach should combine strategic planning, adaptation, cultural understanding, and collaboration with local and international partners. In order to ensure the continued efficacy and success of occupying forces, logisticians play a critical role in addressing the myriad of logistical challenges that they face. Despite the fact that military operations are always evolving, the capacity to overcome logistical obstacles continues to be a crucial factor in determining the success of a mission.

6.2 Afghanistan's harsh climate and its impact on occupiers

Since the beginning of time, Afghanistan's military activities within its borders have been significantly impacted by the country's extremely rough terrain and severe environment. The varied topography of the country presents invading forces with a variety of problems, ranging from sweltering deserts to towering mountain ranges. The purpose of this investigation is to investigate the influence that Afghanistan's harsh environment has on military plans, logistical operations, and the health and safety of occupying personnel.

Diversity According to Geography:

Extremities are a defining characteristic of Afghanistan's geographical variety. The country is home to some of the most imposing mountain ranges in the world, including the Hindu Kush, as well as expansive deserts and plateaus at high altitudes. The climate is characterized by a wide range of variations among regions, with dry and semi-arid conditions in the south and harsh winters in the middle and northern regions. These geographical elements contribute to the widespread variation in climate.

Temperatures That Are Extreme:

The high temperatures that are seen in Afghanistan are one of the most notable characteristics of the country's climate. Temperatures that go considerably above 100 degrees Fahrenheit (38 degrees Celsius) are not uncommon during the summer months in the southern and western regions of the United States. Hot weather can be quite uncomfortable. During the summer, the severity of the heat presents a significant problem for military troops, as it has an influence on their physical endurance, the functionality of their equipment, and their overall effectiveness in their operations.

On the other hand, winters in Afghanistan can be quite cold, especially in the hilly regions (especially the mountains). As a result of the heavy snowfall and cold temperatures that occur in high-altitude regions, logistical operations are made more difficult, and it is difficult for occupying forces to traverse and maintain their equipment.

Obstacles Posed by Altitude:

The hilly geography of the country, which has an average elevation of more than 6,000 feet, poses a one-of-a-kind set of problems for those who are occupying territories. There is a possibility that high altitudes will have a substantial influence on the performance of both workers and machinery. The lower oxygen levels that are present at higher elevations have an impact on the physical well-being of the troops, which may result in altitude sickness and a reduction in the effectiveness of their operations.

There is a possibility that military aircraft and equipment that are designed for use at lower elevations will work less effectively in the thin air that prevails in the mountainous regions of Afghanistan. In order to guarantee functioning and efficiency at different altitudes, it is required to make adjustments and alterations to the equipment. This adds an additional layer of complexity to the operations of the military.

Sandstorms and Dust Storms can occur

Sandstorms and dust storms are common in the arid and semi-arid parts of Afghanistan. These locations are prone to frequent dust storms. These natural occurrences have the potential to significantly restrict visibility, interfere with communication networks, and adversely affect the performance of electronic devices. It is necessary to do routine maintenance on machinery because sand and dust can penetrate it and cause wear and tear.

The unexpected arrival of severe storms is something that occupying troops have to deal with, and it can have an effect on both the planning and execution of military operations. There are hurdles that must be overcome by ground personnel, aircraft, and logistical supply networks in order to successfully navigate through such extreme weather circumstances.

Managing Logistical Obstacles:

When it comes to logistics, the harsh climate of Afghanistan offers a difficult task for the occupiers. It becomes a difficult challenge to maintain a supply chain that is constant and trustworthy, particularly in locations that are more remote and difficult to access. Temperatures that are extremely high, terrain that is difficult to navigate, and weather conditions that are unpredictable all require specialist equipment and transit options.

Being able to transport supplies, fuel, and equipment through hilly terrain and across large deserts demands careful preparation and the capacity to adapt to changing circumstances. A lack of appropriate planning for logistics can result in delays, disruptions in supply, and an increased susceptibility to hostile activities.

The Effect on the Well-Being of Occupiers:

Both the physical and mental well-being of occupying forces in Afghanistan is negatively impacted by the severe weather conditions that prevail there. Frustration, stress, and an overall decrease in combat efficiency are all factors that can be attributed to prolonged exposure to severe weather conditions, high altitudes, and extreme temperatures.

Military troops are exposed to a variety of occupational dangers, including heat-related illnesses during the scorching summers and cold injuries during the hard winters. These hazards become actual problems for them. It is essential for soldiers stationed in Afghanistan to possess the qualities of adaptability and resilience since they are required to navigate and function effectively in an environment that is both cruel and physically demanding.

The severe environment of Afghanistan is a significant aspect that will play a significant role in determining the dynamics of military operations for occupying forces. Extreme temperatures, high altitudes, dust storms, and hard terrains all provide tremendous problems that have an impact on the performance of equipment, the well-being of military personnel, and the logistics of moving supplies and personnel.

For the purpose of adjusting to and minimizing the effects of Afghanistan's climate, strategic planning, specialized equipment, and an in-depth study of the geographical and meteorological nuances are required. As military personnel engage in operations within this hard environment, it is crucial to recognize and manage the effects of the severe climate on occupants. This is necessary in order to preserve operational effectiveness and ensure the welfare of the men and women who are serving in uniform.

Chapter 7

Geopolitical Complexity

When it comes to defining the global stage, the word "geopolitical complexity" encapsulates the dense network of interactions, relationships, and power dynamics that make up the global stage. It is vital to have a solid awareness of the geopolitical environment in order to have a complete comprehension of the factors that influence international relations in this period that is marked by interconnection and interdependence. The purpose of this investigation is to investigate the various aspects of geopolitical complexity by analyzing historical precedents, contemporary issues, and the ever-changing nature of global power dynamics.

Considering the Geopolitical Complexity from a Historical Perspective:

Scholars who were interested in gaining an understanding of the impact that geography has on political affairs gave rise to the subject of study known as geopolitics throughout the latter half of the 19th century and the early 20th century. A number of influential individuals, like Sir Halford Mackinder and Alfred Mahan, were instrumental in the development of geopolitical theory. These individuals placed an emphasis on the role of geographical relationships, natural resources, and strategic positions in determining the distribution of power among nations.

In the course of the two World Wars, geopolitical ideas were put to the test in crucibles, which brought to light the significance of territorial control, access to important resources, and strategic alliances. During the period that followed World War II, the United States and the Soviet Union were engaged in a geopolitical standoff known as the Cold War. This conflict served to further highlight the intricacies of the power relations that exist on a global scale.

There was a significant turning point in geopolitics when the Soviet Union fell apart in 1991. This event led to the establishment of a unipolar international order, with the United States of America serving as the preeminent superpower. With that being said, the 21st century has seen the birth of new geopolitical actors, the resurgence of regional powers, and the expansion of non-state actors, all of which have contributed to the introduction of a new layer of complexity into the realm of international relations.

In the present day, geopolitical challenges include:

The transformation of the international order from a unipolar to a multipolar one has been a distinguishing characteristic of contemporary geopolitics. This transformation has also been accompanied by the rise of regional powers.

China, India, and Brazil are examples of emerging powers that have demonstrated their ability to exert influence on a global and regional scale. The growth of these regional powers brings about a complicated interplay of interests, alliances, and rivalries, which existing countries need to navigate with caution in order to avoid any potential complications.

Interdependence in the Economy and Globalization: The interconnectivity of economies has resulted in the creation of a web of interdependence, in which acts in one region of the world can have far-reaching implications throughout the entire world. When it comes to the formation of geopolitical plans, economic considerations play a vital part, and the integration of global markets brings about new aspects to the dynamics of power. There are a number of factors that contribute to the complexity of international relations, including trade conflicts, economic penalties, and financial vulnerabilities.

In the context of asymmetric warfare, non-state actors:

In addition to the relationships between nation-states, geopolitical complexity includes other factors. Terrorist organizations, multinational companies, and other non-governmental organizations (NGOs) are examples of non-state entities that have the ability to exercise influence on the international stage. Asymmetric warfare, which is defined by unusual tactics utilized by non-state players, challenges traditional concepts of combat. In order to be effective in addressing security threats, it is necessary to employ adaptable techniques and to collaborate with international actors.

Cybersecurity and Technological Advancements: The advent of the digital era has ushered in a new field of geopolitical struggle that is oriented around technology. There are a number of factors that add to the complexity of international relations, including the competition for technological domination, state-sponsored hacking, and cybersecurity. In order to address the ethical, legal, and strategic consequences of developing technologies like artificial intelligence, quantum computing, and biotechnology, nations need to engage in conversations about these issues.

Climate change and resource scarcity are two environmental concerns that overlap with geopolitical factors. Climate change and resource shortage are particularly problematic. The competition for access to vital resources, such as water and energy, can make regional tensions even more pronounced. In addition, the geopolitical consequences of climate-induced migration and the susceptibility of specific regions to changes in the environment bring about new dynamics in the dynamics of global power relations.

Security Conundrums and Arms Races: The pursuit of security by one nation can result in a perceived threat by other nations, which can contribute to security conundrums and arms races. The development of nuclear weapons, territory disputes, and military buildups all contribute to the creation of complex security landscapes that require diplomatic dexterity to administer. Some examples of the difficulties that can arise when attempting to navigate security problems include geopolitical conflicts in locations such as the South China Sea and the Korean Peninsula.

The Changing Characteristics of Power Dynamics on a Global Scale:

The rise of China: The elevation of China to the position of a global economic and military power has resulted in a transformation of the geopolitical landscape. There are a number of factors that contribute to China's influence, including the Belt and Road Initiative (BRI), China's assertiveness in territorial issues in the region, and China's technological breakthroughs. Beijing is becoming more assertive and self-assured, and the international community is struggling to come to terms with the ramifications of this development. China is currently working to redefine its role in global governance.

Great Power Competition Has Been Revisited The 21st century has witnessed a revival of great power competition, with geopolitical tensions between the United States of America, China, and Russia becoming more intense. Technological advancement, military prowess, and the ability to exert influence over international organizations are all examples of areas in which strategic competition is played out. A delicate diplomatic task lies in the management of these rivalry while simultaneously avoiding conflict resolution.

Changes in Alliances and Partnerships There have been changes in conventional alliances as well as the establishment of new partnerships as a result of the geopolitical dynamics that have occurred. When it was first established, the North Atlantic Treaty Organization (NATO) was primarily concerned with the Cold War. The changing form of geopolitical partnerships is reflected in the emerging character of regional alliances in Asia, such as the Quad, which comprises the United States of America, Japan, India, and Australia.

Multilateralism and Global Governance: The necessity of global cooperation in order to address transnational concerns has brought to light the significance of multilateral institutions. Nevertheless, effective global administration is frequently hampered by the intricacies of geopolitical situations, competing interests, and power struggles. Reforms in institutions such as the United states are topics of discussion as states strive to establish an international order that is more inclusive and representative of their interests.

Crisis Management and Soft Power: The intersection of geopolitics and humanitarian crises has a significant impact on the way in which governments and international organizations react to these conflicts.

The ability to influence others by appeal and persuasion rather than through force is referred to as soft power. This ability becomes an essential instrument in the process of influencing worldwide perceptions. It is necessary to have a deep understanding of cultural, economic, and diplomatic elements in order to make effective use of soft power effectively.

Pandemics and the National Security of Global Health The COVID-19 pandemic has brought to light the interconnection of global health and geopolitics. In order to effectively combat pandemics, international collaboration, the exchange of knowledge, and the equitable allocation of resources are all necessary components. The efficiency of global responses to health emergencies is impacted by geopolitical concerns, which have an effect on topics such as the delivery of vaccines and the cooperation in public health projects.

The present international landscape is characterized by a multiplicity of factors —including geopolitical complexity—that shape the interactions between nations. This complexity is a hallmark of the contemporary international landscape. At the same time that present difficulties highlight the complexities that policymakers, diplomats, and strategists must deal with, historical viewpoints offer insights into the development of geopolitical thought.

The dynamic character of global power dynamics, which is being pushed by the growth of regional powers, economic interconnectedness, technological advancements, and environmental issues, necessitates an approach to international relations that is nuanced and adaptable. It is necessary to demonstrate a dedication to diplomacy, multilateralism, and the acknowledgment of shared interests that extend beyond national boundaries in order to successfully navigate this complexity.

The necessity of working together to find answers to geopolitical problems is becoming more and more obvious as the world struggles to deal with these concerns. In order to effectively address concerns such as climate change, economic inequality, and global health, it is necessary to engage in collaborative action and to reimagine international relations in light of the ever-increasing complexity of the situation. The way forward is to cultivate a culture of collaboration, to embrace variety, and to locate areas of common ground in order to construct a global order that is more stable and secure.

7.1 Afghanistan's strategic position in regional geopolitics

Because of its strategic location in the middle of Asia, Afghanistan has been a focal point of geopolitical activity in the region for a very long time. Afghanistan is situated in a geographically distinct region that is surrounded by Central Asia, South Asia, and the Middle East. This position has not only played a significant role in shaping Afghanistan's own destiny, but it has also had an impact on the strategies and interests of surrounding and global powers. The purpose of this investigation is to investigate the strategic relevance of Afghanistan by analyzing historical settings, contemporary issues, and the implications for the stability of the area.

In the context of history:

Afghanistan has been a battleground for conflicting interests and a crossroads for empires on multiple occasions during the course of its history. The geopolitical fight that took place in the 19th century between the Russian Empire and the British Empire for dominance over Central Asia was known as the Great Game. During this conflict, the region's strategic significance became widely apparent. It was essential to achieve Afghanistan's independence in order to preserve the delicate balance of power that existed between the two powers. Afghanistan acted as a buffer zone between them.

The United States of America and the Soviet Union were engaged in a competition for influence in Afghanistan during the 20th century, and Afghanistan once again became a stage for the Cold War competition. An important turning point occurred in 1979 when the Soviet Union invaded Afghanistan. This invasion brought together global entities such as the United States of America, Pakistan, and provincial mujahideen factions, creating a complicated web of alliances and rivalries around the conflict.

Dynamics of the Contemporary Geopolitical System:

The Central Asian Republics that Afghanistan shares borders with include Tajikistan, Uzbekistan, and Turkmenistan, among others. Afghanistan is a bordering country with these Central Asian Republics. The stability of Afghanistan is extremely important for these countries because it has an effect on the state of security in the region, trade routes, and the movement of both people and products. As a result of the fact that instability in Afghanistan has the potential to spread to other parts of the area and cause further instability, Central Asian countries have historically been concerned about the situation in Afghanistan.

South Asian Dynamics: The proximity of Afghanistan to South Asia, with borders that are next to Pakistan and India, lends another layer to the geopolitical relevance of what is happening in Afghanistan. There has been a manifestation of the Indo-Pakistan rivalry in Afghanistan, with both countries attempting to exert influence in order to secure strategic advantages. Establishing peace in Afghanistan is absolutely necessary in order to forestall the propagation of extremism and to guarantee the safety of the South Asian area as a whole.

Afghanistan is a doorway to the Middle East, connecting South Asia and the Middle East. Afghanistan is a gateway to the Middle East. Because of its advantageous location, it has the potential to serve as a corridor for energy pipelines and commercial routes that connect the energy-rich Middle East with markets in South Asia and beyond. It is possible that the stability of these critical economic corridors could be affected by any disruption that occurs in Afghanistan.

The Belt and Road Initiative (BRI) of China: Afghanistan's strategic position crosses with China's ambitious Belt and Road Initiative, which aims to improve connectivity and trade connections. Afghanistan, which is located in close proximity to the province of Xinjiang in China, has the potential to contribute to the expansion of the Belt and Road Initiative (BRI), which will connect Central Asia and South Asia. The success of such connection projects is directly proportional to the degree of stability that exists in Afghanistan.

In the fight against terrorism and extremism, the region surrounding Afghanistan has been a breeding ground for both of these types of extremism and terrorism. The presence of terrorist organizations such as the Taliban and, more recently, the Islamic State of Iraq and the Levant (ISIS) has repercussions on both the regional and global levels. There is a vested interest on the part of neighboring countries, particularly Pakistan and India, to prevent the spread of extremism and to make certain that Afghanistan does not become a safe haven for terrorist activity.

Minerals and rare earth elements are among the natural resources that Afghanistan possesses in abundance. The country also possesses a huge economic potential. Putting these resources to use has the potential to completely alter the economic landscape of the country and to entice investments from other countries. It is important to note, however, that the actualization of this potential is dependent upon the attainment of stability and the establishment of an environment that is favorable to economic development.

Afghanistan's Strategic Significance Faces the Following Obstacles:

Instability Within Afghanistan: Afghanistan's strategic relevance has been confronted with daunting obstacles due to the country's protracted conflict, governmental instability, and ongoing internal turmoil. In an endeavor to construct a state that is stable and coherent, efforts have been hampered by the presence of a number of different factions, the dynamics of tribal groups, and the rebirth of the Taliban.

Afghanistan has been a battleground for a number of different insurgent organizations, each of which has its own unique set of goals and allegiances. Proxy warfare has also been a factor in this conflict environment. The security landscape has become more complicated as a result of the engagement of external actors in providing support to proxy groups.

A fundamental obstacle that still has to be overcome is achieving a balance between the influence of regional powers and minimizing the impact of proxy warfare.

Crisis in Humanitarian Affairs and Migration: Afghanistan is currently experiencing a humanitarian crisis as a result of decades of fighting, which has been aggravated by environmental issues. As a consequence of this, there has been a significant displacement of people and waves of refugees seeking asylum in nations that are nearby. Because surrounding countries are forced to deal with the social, economic, and security ramifications of large-scale migration, the humanitarian factor adds an additional degree of complexity to the geopolitical situation in the region.

Historically, Afghanistan has been a significant producer of opium, which has allowed it to make a contribution to the international narcotics trade. The illegal drug trade not only contributes to the escalation of domestic conflict, but it also has repercussions for the security of both the region and the world. The international community, which includes nations that are geographically close to Afghanistan, has a common interest in tackling the fundamental factors that contribute to the manufacturing and trafficking of narcotics that originate from Afghanistan.

Possibilities for Cooperation throughout the Region:

Diplomatic Engagement: The intricate geopolitical dynamics that surround Afghanistan call for diplomatic engagement and conversation among the various nations in the region. Assisting in the resolution of conflicts and promoting regional stability can be accomplished through the establishment of communication channels and the promotion of diplomatic initiatives.

Economic connection: Because of its advantageous location, Afghanistan has the potential to become a hub for economic connection, which would make it easier for Afghanistan to facilitate commerce and transit between Central Asia, South Asia, and the Middle East. The region's economic potential can be unlocked through the establishment of trade corridors and the development of infrastructure through regional collaboration.

The importance of regional cooperation in the areas of intelligence sharing, border control, and counterterrorism tactics cannot be overstated in light of the fact that there is a common interest in combating terrorism and extremism. Afghanistan and the region as a whole can benefit from the stability that can be achieved through the implementation of a collaborative strategy to solve security concerns.

Humanitarian Assistance and Development: Regional collaboration on initiatives including humanitarian assistance and development can be an effective means of addressing the underlying factors that contribute to instability. Long-term stability and resilience can be contributed to by collaborative efforts to enhance living conditions, give educational chances, and provide economic prospects.

Cooperation in Environmental Matters: In order to address environmental concerns, such as the lack of available water and the effects of climate change, regional cooperation is required. When it comes to ensuring sustainable development and mitigating possible sources of conflict, collaborative solutions are required since shared resources and environmental risks force people to work together.

The important position that Afghanistan holds in the geopolitical landscape of the area constitutes both a source of problems and possibilities. The intricacy of Afghanistan's role in defining the geopolitical landscape of Central Asia, South Asia, and the Middle East is highlighted by the historical setting of the Great Game and the Cold War, as well as by the dynamics that are occurring in the present day.

Recognizing the common interests of regional countries, fostering diplomatic initiatives, and engaging in cooperative efforts to address common difficulties are all necessary steps on the route forward. It is possible for neighboring countries and the international community to make a contribution to a more secure and prosperous future for the region by capitalizing on Afghanistan's strategic location for economic connectivity, combating terrorism, and fostering regional security. A sophisticated and collaborative strategy that goes beyond immediate geopolitical concerns is required in order to handle the many issues that Afghanistan and its neighbors are currently facing. This is because the complexity that is inherent in Afghanistan's strategic significance need such an approach.

7.2 The influence of neighboring countries on resistance efforts

Whether they are directed against a foreign occupation, oppressive regimes, or ideological enemies, resistance movements are influenced by a complex interplay of internal dynamics and external factors. For a variety of reasons, including their proximity to one another geographically and their strategic interests, neighboring countries frequently play a vital role in either supporting or challenging resistance movements. An examination of historical precedents, geopolitical concerns, and the ramifications for the success or failure of resistance activities are included in this investigation, which digs into the myriad of ways in which neighboring nations exert impact on resistance attempts.

Perspectives on the Past: historic

There have been numerous instances throughout history in which neighboring countries have had influence over resistance attempts. There have been a variety of conflicts, ranging from anti-colonial campaigns to movements against authoritarian regimes, in which neighboring nations have played a significant role in either supporting or suppressing resistance movements. One example that is particularly noteworthy is the assistance that neighboring countries offered to the French Resistance during World War II. During this time, Allied nations, particularly the United Kingdom, played a significant role in providing assistance to the resistance in its fight against Nazi occupation.

On the other hand, neighboring countries can also play a role in enabling tyranny, as is evident in situations where authoritarian regimes obtain assistance from their neighbors. Not only did domestic security forces play a role in the suppression of uprisings that occurred during the Arab Spring in countries such as Syria and Bahrain, but regional coalitions that aimed to uphold the status quo were also involved.

Take into account geopolitical factors:

Alliances Strategic: Countries that are geographically close to one another may form strategic alliances with resistance organizations on the basis of their common geopolitical objectives. Support from neighboring nations can take the shape of diplomatic backing, military help, or the provision of safe havens for resistance leaders and fighters. All of these forms of support are possible. On the other hand, geopolitical reasons may cause neighboring nations to oppose resistance attempts, particularly if the movement poses a challenge to the established power relations in the region.

The proximity of resistance groups to neighboring nations provides them with the opportunity to establish refuge and support bases because of their proximity to these countries. It is possible that neighboring countries may provide resistance fighters with safe havens, training grounds, and logistical support at their disposal. As an illustration, the Afghan resistance against Soviet occupation in the 1980s sought refuge and support in Pakistan, whilst the Tamil Tigers in Sri Lanka gained backing from sympathetic elements in India. Both of these groups were fighting against the Soviet rule of Afghanistan.

Recruitment of Fighters and the Movement of Resources Across Borders: Countries that are geographically close to one another can make it easier to recruit fighters and to move resources across borders. Because of this assistance, resistance movements have the potential to greatly improve their capabilities. It was the Kurdish communities in neighboring Iran and Turkey that provided support for the Kurdish resistance against Saddam Hussein's administration in Iraq, which contributed to the movement's durability.

Counterinsurgency Efforts: On the other hand, surrounding countries may work along with the occupying force or the oppressive regime in order to fight the efforts of the resistance. The suppression of the resistance may be accomplished through this collaboration through the exchange of intelligence, the conduct of coordinated military actions, or the supply of financial and logistical support. These kinds of activities could be motivated by a desire to preserve stability, to safeguard economic interests, or to coincide with the political philosophy of the oppressor.

One example of the influence of neighboring countries on resistance efforts is as follows:

Pakistan, which was a nearby country and became a crucial actor in the anti-Soviet insurgency, provided substantial support to the Afghan resistance, which was known as the Mujahideen, during the Soviet-Afghan War (1979-1989). Through the country of Pakistan, the United States of America and Saudi Arabia supplied major financial and military assistance to the Mujahideen. The success of the resistance movement in compel the Soviet Union to withdraw from the region had long-lasting repercussions for the area, and it was a major factor in the final collapse of the Soviet Union.

The Syrian Civil War (2011-present): The conflict in Syria has seen neighboring countries play a variety of roles in influencing the efforts of the resistance. Iran has supplied major support to the Syrian government, while Turkey has sponsored a variety of rebel forces that are opposed to the administration of Assad. The participation of regional and global powers, each of which has its own set of interests and alliances, has added to the complexity of the geopolitical scene, which has had an effect on the course of the resistance in Syria as well as the results of the conflict.

Conflict between Israel and Palestine The Israeli-Palestinian conflict is characterized by the involvement of surrounding Arab countries in either supporting or opposing Palestinian resistance groups. Iran and a few Arab states have been among the nations that have offered financial and military assistance to terrorist organizations like Hamas and Hezbollah. On the other hand, other nations, particularly those that are active in peace negotiations, have been looking for diplomatic solutions. Throughout the course of this lengthy battle, one of the most consistent characteristics has been the effect of neighboring nations on the resistance.

The conflict in Eastern Ukraine, particularly in Donetsk and Luhansk, has seen involvement from Russia, which is located in close proximity to Ukraine. This conflict began in 2014 and continues to this day. There is evidence that implies Russia is supporting separatist movements, despite the fact that Russia denies any direct military participation. On the other hand, the battle highlights the impact that geopolitical considerations and the influence of neighboring countries have on the dynamics of resistance activities.

Possible Consequences for Movements of Resistance:

The power and resilience of resistance movements can be considerably bolstered by the support they receive from countries that are geographically close to them. An increase in the movement's military capabilities and its capacity to survive counterinsurgency measures can be achieved through the provision of money, safe havens, and assistance from beyond international borders.

Vulnerability and Isolation: On the other hand, resistance groups may be left vulnerable and isolated if they do not receive support from adjacent nations or if they face direct opposition from those governments. When movements do not receive support from outside sources, they may have difficulty maintaining their own existence, encounter difficulties in recruiting and organizing members, and have a difficult time gaining international legitimacy.

Regionalization of Conflicts: Countries that are geographically close to one another have the potential to play a role in the regionalization of conflicts, which can transform isolated resistance movements into more widespread geopolitical confrontations. It is possible for this regionalization to exacerbate existing conflicts, make diplomatic attempts more difficult, and result in greater instability that has ramifications that extend beyond the immediate theater of resistance.

The influence of neighboring nations on resistance activities has substantial consequences for peace processes. This influence can be seen as a significant impact on peace processes. It is possible for a resistance movement to be able to negotiate from a position of strength with the assistance of external backing; but, this can also prolong conflicts if the nations that are bordering the movement are not dedicated to peaceful outcomes. Diplomatic endeavors can be successful or unsuccessful depending on whether they are based on regional cooperation or competition.

Within the realm of geopolitical dynamics, one of the most dynamic and complicated aspects is the influence that neighboring countries have on resistance attempts. The examples, both historical and present, highlight the myriad of ways in which neighboring nations have the ability to influence the manner in which resistance groups develop themselves. When it comes to determining the fate of resistance struggles, the role of neighboring countries is crucial. This can be accomplished by strategic alliances, military backing, cross-border resources, or counterinsurgency efforts from the bordering countries.

To successfully navigate the geopolitical landscape, resistance groups need to have a solid awareness of potential sources of support and the ability to leverage those sources while also limiting the problems that are offered by opposition or isolation.

When it comes to devising successful ways to address disputes, promote peace, and preserve stability in regions that are marked by resistance activities, it is essential for policymakers and analysts to acknowledge the influence of neighboring states. Resistance movements are intricate components of the larger geopolitical tapestry because of the interplay between internal dynamics and external forces. This interplay highlights the intricacy of resistance movements.

Chapter 8

Lessons Learned and Modern Context

The dynamic nature of the modern world presents a pattern of opportunities and challenges that is always shifting and evolving. In a time when societies are struggling to adapt to a wide range of complex concerns, including technological breakthroughs, geopolitical shifts, and global health crises, the lessons that have been learned from past events serve as guiding lights of wisdom. This investigation dives into the lessons that have been learned from the past and how they might be applied in the present day. It places an emphasis on the necessity of adaptable techniques and inventive ways in order to address the myriad of issues that the 21st century presents.

Lessons Learned from the Past:

Characteristics of Adaptability in the Face of Change: Throughout the course of human history, civilizations that have shown the ability to adapt to change have flourished. One of the most important factors that has determined success throughout history, from the Industrial Revolution to the Information Age, has been the capacity to accept and embrace technological developments and economic transformations. The takeaway from this is crystal clear: individuals and organizations that are resistant to change run the risk of becoming stagnant, whereas those that are able to adapt are able to harness the force of innovation.

The Importance of Global Cooperation The lessons that may be learned from events such as the establishment of the United Nations during World War II highlight the crucial role that global cooperation plays in tackling issues that are shared by countries all over the world. These days, problems like climate change, pandemics, and cyber threats are not limited to a single nation's boundaries; therefore, it is essential to work together and combine efforts from multiple countries. The success of multinational efforts is contingent on a collaborative commitment to bettering the well-being of the group as a whole.

Resilience in the Face of Adversity: Resilience has been a recurrent topic throughout the history of humanity, starting from the process of rebuilding after wars to the process of recovering from economic downturns. In the present setting, where communities are confronted with unprecedented challenges, such as natural disasters, political upheavals, and global crises, the ability to recover quickly from adversity is of the utmost importance. In order for communities to be able to weather storms and emerge stronger, it is necessary to construct resilient systems.

Maintaining a Balance Between Ethical Issues and Technological Progress The lessons that were learnt from the tremendous advancements that occurred during the industrial and digital ages show how important it is to maintain a balance between technological progress and ethical issues. Ethical frameworks and responsible innovation are needed in order to avert unexpected consequences and protect human rights as cutting-edge technologies such as artificial intelligence, biotechnology, and others continue to transform societies.

Governance that is inclusive for the purpose of achieving social stability The historical struggles for civil rights and social justice highlight the significance of inclusive governance. Social stability is more likely to be achieved by societies that prioritize equality, fairness, and inclusiveness in their policies and practices. In order to ensure that various perspectives are heard and that policies reflect the interests of all sectors of society, the current setting necessitates a reevaluation of the structures that govern the society.

Contemporary Context:

Disruption in Technology and Ethical Considerations The rapid speed of technical innovation in the modern period, which includes breakthroughs in artificial intelligence, biotechnology, and cybersecurity, requires a watchful approach to ethical considerations. Such an approach is necessary because of the potential for technological disruption. The unfettered pursuit of technical development at the price of privacy, security, and ethical norms is something that should be avoided at all costs, according to the lessons learned from the past. It is absolutely necessary to engage in responsible innovation that takes into account the wider societal impact.

Global Health Challenges and Preparedness The lessons that have been learnt from previous pandemics, such as the Spanish flu, as well as more recent outbreaks, such as Ebola and H1N1, highlight the significance of being prepared for global health emergencies. As a result of the COVID-19 pandemic, weaknesses in public health systems have been brought to light, and the necessity of coordinated worldwide responses has been brought to light. Important lessons for the present day include the strengthening of healthcare infrastructure, the collaboration of researchers from throughout the world, and the provision of vaccines to everyone who needs them.

Environmental Sustainability and Climate Action: The environmental lessons that have been learned from industrialization and unfettered resource exploitation highlight the urgent need for behaviors that are sustainable. It is imperative that collective action be taken in order to alleviate the effects of climate change, which poses an existential threat. When it comes to preserving the world for future generations, the lessons that may be learned from environmental degradation in the past highlight the significance of conservation, utilization of renewable energy sources, and international collaboration.

Shifts in the Geopolitical Landscape and Diplomacy The geopolitical landscape is in a state of perpetual flux, with power dynamics moving across international nations. The importance of successful diplomacy in settling disputes and developing international collaboration is highlighted by the lessons that may be learned from historical conflicts, tensions during the Cold War, and diplomatic breakthroughs. Given the current circumstances, it is necessary to be able to navigate geopolitical obstacles with skill in order to collaboratively handle global issues.

Inclusivity and Social Justice Movements: Contemporary social justice movements, which are a reflection of the fights that have occurred in the past, place an emphasis on the necessity of inclusiveness, equality, and justice. The lessons that have been learnt from civil rights movements, campaigning for women's rights, and advocacy for LGBTQ+ individuals highlight the significance of eliminating pervasive disparities in society. In order to construct communities that are both robust and peaceful, contemporary cultures must continue to work toward achieving social fairness and inclusivity.

Cybersecurity Challenges and Digital Resilience: As societies become more dependent on digital technology, the lessons that may be learned from previous breaches and cyberattacks highlight the importance of implementing robust cybersecurity safeguards. Given the ever-evolving nature of cyber threats, it is of the utmost importance to ensure the protection of key infrastructure, the protection of personal data, and the development of digital resilience.

When it comes to managing the intricacies of the current world, the lessons that may be gleaned from history provide absolutely priceless insights. There is a wealth of knowledge that may be gleaned from the past to influence decision-making in the present day. This knowledge can range from flexibility and global cooperation to ethical considerations and social fairness. Considering that societies are currently facing issues that have never been seen before, the capacity to combine historical lessons with creative ways is of the utmost importance.

Resilience, flexibility, and ethical considerations are essential pillars for sustainable success in the current setting, which is characterized by a much faster pace of innovation. When it comes to confronting technology shocks, global health crises, environmental problems, or geopolitical shifts, the lessons that have been learnt from the annals of history serve as a compass for charting a course toward a future that is more egalitarian, resilient, and peaceful. Societies are able to negotiate the evolving landscape of global difficulties and carve a path toward a future that is more sustainable and inclusive if they combine the wisdom of the past with methods that are forward-thinking.

8.1 Insights from historical events

Documenting victories, tragedies, and the development of societies, the chronicles of history serve as a rich tapestry of human experiences. A rich tapestry of human experiences. The insights that can be gained from historical events give essential lessons that can be used to guide decision-making and inform modern thinking. The purpose of this investigation is to look into the profound insights that may be gained by examining historical events, with a particular emphasis on the significance of these insights in making sense of the difficulties of the present and constructing a more enlightened future.

A lesson that will last a lifetime is the realization that power is ephemeral. This is one of the lessons that history has taught us. The rise and fall of empires, the emergence and collapse of major civilizations, and the tremendous shifts that political systems go through are all examples. An understanding of the cyclical nature of power dynamics can be gained via the study of the development and fall of ancient civilizations, such as the Roman Empire. A contemporary leader is encouraged to approach governance with a feeling of responsibility and adaptability when they have the understanding that no power system is immune to change. This understanding also creates humility with contemporary leaders.

The Influence of Ideological Shifts The transformative force of ideological shifts is frequently demonstrated by incidents that occurred in the past time period. Throughout the course of human history, revolutions such as the French Revolution and the Industrial Revolution have had a significant impact on that course. The realizations that were attained as a result of these occurrences emphasize the impact that ideas have on the systems of societies, economies, and governments. Understanding the influence of ideological shifts is essential for forecasting societal changes and designing futures that are inclusive, equitable, and sustainable in today's world, at a time when ideologies are still in the process of continuous evolution.

The Consequences of strife: The wars and conflicts that have occurred throughout history offer important insights into the destructive consequences that are associated with human strife. The lessons that can be learned from the World Wars, the Cold War, and regional wars illustrate the extent of the damage that has been done to human lives, economy, and connections between nations. The study of these events highlights the importance of diplomacy, the resolution of conflicts, and the pursuit of peace. The wounds left by past wars serve as powerful reminders of the importance of putting an emphasis on communication and collaboration in order to address the difficulties that are facing the world today.

One of the most powerful aspects of history is the ability of individuals, communities, and nations to persevere in the face of hardship. Historical events frequently demonstrate this extraordinary resilience.

The experiences of people who have overcome adversity, whether it be natural disasters, economic downturns, or political upheavals, serve as a source of motivation towards conquering modern issues. By gaining an understanding of the characteristics that enable resilience, such as adaptability, solidarity, and inventiveness, one can get significant insights that can be utilized in the construction of strong societies that are able to navigate uncertainty.

The Intersection of Cultural trade: Throughout the course of human history, cultures have come into contact with one another, which has resulted in periods of lively and mutually influential trade. There have been periods of cultural interchange that have contributed to the development of human civilization, such as the Silk Road, the Renaissance, and the Age of Exploration. Insights gained from these historical exchanges highlight the importance of diversity, cultural understanding, and the advantages of collaboration in terms of encouraging creativity, intellectual growth, and societal advancement.

Insights into the dynamics of wealth and inequality can be gained via the study of economic changes. These transformations, which range from the Agricultural Revolution to the Information Age, offer valuable experiences and lessons. A number of historical occurrences, including the Great Depression and the Industrial Revolution, highlight the need of economic systems that strike a balance between economic growth and social welfare provisions. The modern efforts to construct inclusive, sustainable economies that promote the well-being of all citizens are informed by an understanding of the lessons that can be learned from the experiences of economic history.

Throughout history, there have been numerous movements that have fought for human rights. These movements include the civil rights movement, the women's suffrage movement, and the anti-apartheid campaign. These movements have provided valuable lessons that can be applied to the continuous quest for justice and equality. The lessons that may be learned from these movements emphasize the significance of solidarity, the strength of grassroots engagement, and the requirement of confronting injustices that are embedded in various systems. The present efforts that are being made to address issues of discrimination, inequality, and violations of human rights are strengthened by these teachings.

Historic events also shed light on the impact that human actions have had on the ecosystem, which is an important aspect of environmental stewardship. The lessons that have been learnt from the environmental degradation that has occurred throughout history highlight the critical need for sustainable practices. These lessons range from deforestation to industrial pollution. Contemporary environmental stewardship efforts are informed by the lessons learned from the consequences of unregulated exploitation of natural resources. These lessons emphasize the significance of responsible resource management and conservation.

A Look at the Impact of Technology on the Transformation of Societies:

One can have a better understanding of the transformational impact of technology by looking at the history of technical breakthroughs, beginning with the invention of the printing press and ending with the digital revolution. Not only can historical events, such as the introduction of the internet, bring to light the possibility of positive change, but they also bring about issues in terms of ethics and society. By gaining an understanding of the historical relationship that existed between technology and society, present conversations about responsible innovation, privacy, and the ethical application of emerging technologies can be informed better.

The dynamics of social movements, such as the struggle for women's rights, the campaign for LGBTQ+ rights, and anti-apartheid demonstrations, offer insights into the power of collective action to promote societal change. Such movements include the demonstrations against apartheid. The lessons that may be learned from these campaigns highlight the significance of grassroots activity, civic involvement, and the perseverance that is necessary to combat deeply ingrained institutionalized forms of mistreatment. The present efforts that are being made to address social disparities and advocate for beneficial societal transitions are significantly influenced by these discoveries.

Applicability to the Present Day:

The modern world is interconnected, as evidenced by the insights gained from historical events, which highlight the interrelated nature of the modern world. Isolationism, nationalism, and ethnocentrism have all had negative effects, and the lessons that have been learnt from those results highlight the significance of global collaboration. In this age of unparalleled connection, it is essential to have a solid understanding of the interdependence of nations in order to effectively manage global difficulties such as pandemics and climate change problems.

In order to successfully navigate the rapid rate of technical breakthroughs that are occurring in the modern period, it is necessary to have a sophisticated awareness of the historical precedents that have been established. Discussions on the ethical implications of artificial intelligence, the influence of automation on employment, and the necessity of responsible innovation are informed by knowledge gained from the technological revolutions that have occurred in the past. Our current efforts to harness technology for the greater good are guided by the lessons that we have learned from the technological revolutions that have occurred throughout history.

In order to promote inclusive governance, it is important to remember that the lessons learned from the past fights for civil rights and inclusive government continue to be extremely relevant.

A commitment to inclusiveness and equal representation is required in order to address the contemporary difficulties that are associated with systematic racism, gender inequality, and institutionalized social injustice. It is through the insights gained from previous movements that efforts are made to construct societies that place a priority on diversity, equity, and social justice.

Environmental Sustainability: At a time when the globe is struggling to cope with the effects of climate change and the destruction of the environment, the lessons that may be learned from past events highlight the critical need for implementation of sustainable practices. Efforts that are currently being made to transition to renewable energy, minimize ecological harm, and develop a more sustainable relationship with the earth are informed by the environmental issues that have occurred in the past.

Concerns Regarding Humanitarian Issues and Global Health The lessons that have been learnt from previous pandemics and humanitarian crises give essential insights that can be used to address modern difficulties and issues pertaining to global health. The pandemic of COVID-19 that is currently going on highlights the significance of worldwide cooperation, preparedness, and equitable access to medical education and treatment. Efforts to strengthen public health systems and promote resilience in the face of rising threats are guided by insights gained from previous emergency situations involving public health.

Cultural Exchange and Diversity: In a world that is defined by several different cultures and communities that are interconnected, the lessons that may be learned from historical cultural exchange continue to be relevant. The contemporary attempts to promote tolerance, cross-cultural understanding, and collaboration are informed by today's efforts to get a knowledge of the good influence that cultural variety has. The historical periods of cultural exchange provide valuable insights that lead to the development of global communities that are both inclusive and peaceful.

Insights gained from past events act as a compass, directing mankind through the complexity of the present and toward a future that is more enlightened. The profound lessons that may be learned from the rise and fall of empires, ideological upheavals, conflicts, resiliency, and societal transformations give wisdom that is eternal. It is impossible to overestimate the significance of historical insights in the modern setting, where the challenges are unprecedented in terms of both magnitude and scope.

It is possible for societies to traverse the challenges of the modern era with knowledge, foresight, and a dedication to constructive change if they draw upon the collective experiences of humanity.

The lessons that we have gained from historical events serve to remind us of the enduring force of human agency, the significance of ethical considerations in the process of invention, and the necessity of global cooperation in the face of challenges that are shared by millions of people. Accepting the lessons that history has to offer gives individuals and society the ability to design a world that is more just, egalitarian, and resilient. This is because we are the guardians of the past, the present, and the future.

8.2 Contemporary resistance movements and global perspectives on occupation

Contemporary resistance movements play a key role in resisting oppressive forces, expressing the rights of oppressed populations, and molding the narrative of occupation by influencing the terrain of global geopolitics, which is constantly shifting and evolving. Whether it is the occupied areas in the Middle East or the efforts for self-determination in diverse regions, these movements are remarkable examples of the human spirit's ability to persevere in the face of insurmountable obstacles. As part of this investigation, the dynamics of modern resistance movements and the worldwide perspectives on occupation are investigated. The motivations, problems, and broader consequences for international relations are also taken into consideration.

Resistance Movements in the Contemporary World:

Struggle for Self-Determination of the Palestinian People The Israeli-Palestinian conflict is largely considered as one of the most durable and publicly recognized modern resistance movements. Against the Israeli occupation of the West Bank, East Jerusalem, and Gaza Strip, the Palestinian people have been engaged in a protracted battle for self-determination. This struggle has been going on for quite some time. The resistance is composed of a wide range of players, ranging from grassroots activists to armed factions, all of whom are motivated by a desire for justice, dignity, and the right to select their own political future.

Kashmiri Independence Movement: In the contested territory of Kashmir, a lengthy battle for independence has been unfolding. This struggle has been distinguished by a complex web of historical, religious, and geopolitical causes. As a result of being caught in the crossfire between India and Pakistan, the people of Kashmir are fighting back against what they consider to be an occupation and a rejection of their right to self-determination. As a result of the battle, which includes both non-violent movements and armed resistance, the complexity of identity, borders, and sovereignty are brought to light.

Issues over the erosion of political liberties and autonomy promised by the "one country, two systems" principle gave rise to the pro-democracy movement in Hong Kong. This movement began as a response to the issues that were raised.

More democratic representation and independence from Beijing's control were among the demands made during demonstrations, which were primarily organized by young people. The movement was subjected to a growing amount of repression, which reflected a worldwide struggle for democratic values in the face of authoritarian inclinations.

The Struggle for Democracy in Myanmar: Myanmar has been witness to persistent struggle against military rule, with pro-democracy movements contesting the dominance of the military junta. The objective of the civil disobedience movement is to bring back democratic governance. This movement is headed by a wide collection of individuals, including students, activists, and members of ethnic minorities. The international community has been paying close attention to the unfolding events in Myanmar, which has brought to light the significance of solidarity in an environment characterized by authoritarianism.

Movement for the Independence of the Western Sahara Because the Western Sahara is a disputed region in North Africa, it has been at the focus of a struggle for independence that has been going on for a very long time. In order to establish their right to self-determination, the indigenous Sahrawi people are fighting against what they perceive to be Moroccan occupation. The conflict is characterized by violent resistance, diplomatic initiatives, and requests for a referendum to be overseen by the United Nations in order to define the status of the region.

Perspectives on Occupation from Around the World:

Concern for Human Rights Violations: The concern for human rights violations in occupied regions is a common thread that runs through modern resistance groups. There are frequent allegations that the occupying forces have engaged in disproportionate use of force, imposed limits on the freedom of movement, and arbitrarily detained individuals. Perspectives from around the world on occupation demonstrate how important it is to preserve international human rights norms and to hold accountable those who are guilty of atrocities.

Laws of the International Community and Resolutions of the United Nations: The observance of international law and the resolutions of the United Nations that are pertinent to the topic of occupation create global attitudes. The freedom of people living in occupied territories to freely select their political status is emphasized by the universally recognized principle of self-determination, which is incorporated in the United Nations Charter. Violations of international law, such as the development of settlements in lands that are occupied, are met with widespread condemnation and calls for accountability.

Diplomatic and Economic Pressures: In order to address occupations and to encourage conflict settlement, the international community frequently applies diplomatic and economic pressures.

This rejection of occupying forces can be communicated through the use of sanctions, diplomatic isolation, and the removal of economic support, among other useful weapons. The implementation of these steps is intended to foster negotiations, dialogue, and respect for international norms.

Civil society and global activism both play an important part in the formation of perspectives on occupation. This is because of the role that they play in helping to shape perspectives. Individuals who have been impacted by occupation are able to have their voices heard through movements that advocate for human rights, justice, and self-determination. In order to raise awareness and mobilize support for the struggle against occupation, international solidarity, which can be represented through protests, advocacy campaigns, and grassroots activities, is a significant contributor.

Influence of the Media and Information Warfare: It is the narratives of the media and information warfare that affect the attitudes of people all over the world regarding occupation. A struggle for public opinion is being waged between occupying troops and resistance movements, with both groups making use of various media outlets to express their respective narratives. In order to provide an accurate perspective of the events that are taking place on the ground and to combat misinformation, the critical role that independent journalism and objective reporting play becomes increasingly important.

Considerations of Geostrategic Implications As a result of powerful states aligning their interests based on regional stability, access to resources, and geopolitical alliances, occupation is frequently regarded through the lens of geostrategic considerations. The complexity of international relations is shown by the fact that the influence of major powers in developing global perceptions on occupation highlights the fact that strategic objectives can sometimes take precedence over values of justice and self-determination for different countries.

Current resistance movements are confronted with the following challenges:

Repression and Crackdowns: Many resistance groups are subjected to repression and crackdowns from the forces who are occupying the territory. These crackdowns can result in arrests, injuries, and restrictions on the freedom of expression. The use of force in a disproportionate manner causes substantial hurdles for prolonged opposition and hinders the ability of movements to generate support from around the world.

Fragmentation and Internal splits: The effectiveness of resistance movements might be hindered by the presence of internal splits and factionalism within those movements. The presence of divergent ideologies, strategies, and objectives can result in fragmentation, which makes it difficult to present a unified front and negotiate from a position of strength.

The influence of global power dynamics, in which powerful states may prioritize geopolitical interests over human rights and self-determination, is a substantial obstacle. This is because of the fact that global power dynamics exist. There is a possibility that resistance movements will have a difficult time gaining real support on the world stage, particularly in situations when major nations side behind the occupying forces.

Disruptions to the Economy and Society: Occupied regions frequently have economic and social disruptions, which have an effect on the living conditions of the people who live there. The economic difficulties, in conjunction with the limits placed on movement, have the potential to produce an atmosphere of dependence and to disrupt the capacity of resistance movements to gather resources for the purpose of maintaining their activism.

Propaganda and Information Warfare: In order to influence public opinion, occupying forces and resistance movements are engaged in a battle for narratives. They are employing propaganda and information warfare in this conflict. There is a possibility that efforts to convey the reality of the situation and to mobilize world-wide assistance may be made more difficult by the proliferation of false information and competing narratives.

At the intersection of human rights, geopolitical considerations, and the quest for justice, contemporary resistance movements and global perspectives on occupation intersect with one another. In the tales of occupied territories, the struggles of communities to express their right to self-determination are reflected. These groups frequently encounter enormous obstacles in their pursuit of this right. The discourse on occupation is influenced by global viewpoints, which are determined by international law, diplomatic forces, and the activism of civil society. These perspectives also contribute to the trajectory where wars are headed.

As the globe continues to struggle with challenges of occupation and resistance, it is becoming increasingly important for the international community to engage in nuanced conversations, putting human rights at the forefront of their concerns, and looking for solutions that are just and equitable. The complex and multi-faceted dialogue that defines the present and shapes the aspirations of a more just and peaceful future is shaped by the lessons learned from historical events, the resiliency of contemporary resistance movements, and the evolving dynamics of global perspectives on occupation. All of these factors contribute collectively to the formation of this dialogue.

Chapter 9

Conclusion

The history of Afghanistan is filled with stories of resiliency, resistance, and unwavering defiance against forces from the outside world. The Afghan people have continually displayed a spirit of resistance that has left an indelible stamp on the nation's identity. This spirit of resistance has been demonstrated throughout the history of Afghanistan, beginning with the period of British colonialism and continuing through the Soviet invasion and the more recent challenges posed by various extremist groups. In this investigation, the conclusion of Afghanistan's historical defiance is investigated. The legacy of resistance, the lessons learned, and the ramifications for the future of the country are all taken into consideration.

Afghanistan's Resistance Leaves Behind:

Colonialism by the British and the Great Game: The history of Afghan resistance may be traced back to the 19th century, at the time of the Great Game, which was a competition between imperial powers for influence in Central Asia. The British attempted to colonize Afghanistan, which is also known as the "Graveyard of Empires," but Afghanistan successfully rejected their efforts. A legacy of resistance against foreign interference was developed as a result of the courageous efforts of Afghan leaders such as Ahmad Shah Durrani and the strategic prowess exhibited throughout the Anglo-Afghan Wars.

On the other hand, the fight against the Soviet invasion that took place in Afghanistan in the latter part of the 20th century is considered to be one of the most important chapters in the country's history. The Mujahideen, a coalition of Afghan resistance forces supported by the United States of America, Saudi Arabia, and Pakistan, came into being during the Soviet-Afghan War, which lasted from 1979 between 1979 and 1989. The people of Afghanistan resisted the Soviet occupation with unyielding tenacity, which finally resulted in the withdrawal of Soviet soldiers and the conclusion of the Cold War era.

Following the withdrawal of Soviet forces from Afghanistan, the country entered a period of internal struggle, which culminated in the establishment of the Taliban in the 1990s. At the same time, the Taliban posed a challenge to the government. Resistance was inspired by the brutal rule of the Taliban, particularly from the Northern Alliance, which was composed of a variety of ethnic and regional groups working together. On the other hand, the struggle against Taliban rule laid the groundwork for the subsequent invasion led by the United States in the early 2000s.

As Afghanistan became a focal point in the global War on Terror, the post-9/11 era witnessed a fresh phase of resistance. This was a direct result of the intervention led by the United States. The people of Afghanistan were confronted with the dual problem of removing the Taliban administration and fighting against the occupation by foreign forces. The construction of democratic institutions and the emergence of a new administration in Afghanistan signaled a shift; nonetheless, opposition to foreign forces and the incursion of extremist ideas continued to exist.

Enduring Struggle Against Extremism: Following the intervention led by the United States, Afghanistan struggled with the emergence of extremist groups, most notably the resurgence of the Taliban. Consistent efforts to combat terrorism and safeguard the progress established in the post-Taliban era were made by the Afghan National Security Forces, which received help from international allies and the international community. As Afghan soldiers remained resilient in the face of the simultaneous challenges of insurgency and terrorism, the heritage of resistance continued from the previous generation.

From Afghanistan's historical defiance, we have learned the following lessons:

Resilience of Local Populations in the Face of Foreign Occupation One of the most important takeaways from Afghanistan's historical defiance is the resilience of local populations in the face of foreign occupation. Despite the repeated attempts by foreign powers to take control over Afghanistan, the Afghan people have consistently resisted these attempts, which highlights the inextricable bond that exists between the Afghan people and their natural environment.

Afghanistan's history is marked by its broad ethnic and tribal makeup, which has contributed to the country's unity in diversity. Even though these disparities exist, there have been instances of historical defiance that have demonstrated instances of togetherness among Afghan groups when they were confronted with external threats. When resistance actions were taking place, the capacity to create coalitions across ethnic lines is a prime example of the strength that may be generated from diversity.

The role of foreign support: Throughout Afghanistan's history, disobedience has frequently been accompanied with backing from outside sources, whether it was during the time of British colonial rule, the Soviet-Afghan War, or subsequent conflicts. In order to strengthen resistance movements against powerful opponents, the lessons learnt highlight the significance of strategic alliances and international backing; these are both essential components.

The internal tensions and disintegration that occurred as a result of the withdrawal of Soviet forces serve as a cautionary story. These consequences will be discussed further in the following paragraphs.

The subsequent power vacuum and internal strife among Afghan factions had a significant role in paving the way for the development of the Taliban, highlighting the need of post-conflict governance and stability.

Impact of Ideological fights The historical defiance of Afghanistan is a reflection of the impact that ideological fights have had on the course of the country. Different ideologies have been a source of contention for the Afghan people throughout their history, from their opposition to Soviet communism to their challenge to the Taliban's stringent interpretation of Islam. When it comes to resolving ideological differences, this experience highlights the need of having a detailed awareness of the dynamics and values of the local community.

There have been serious humanitarian implications as a result of the lengthy periods of conflict in Afghanistan. These effects include the displacement of people, the loss of lives, and the hardships that have been experienced economically. The lessons that were learnt highlight how important it is to prioritize the well-being of civilians, provide relief to those in need, and facilitate attempts to rebuild in order to reduce the negative effects of prolonged conflicts.

Possible Consequences for the Future of Afghanistan:

Quest for Stability and Peace: The historical defiance of Afghanistan serves as the foundation for the ongoing search for stability and peace in the country. It is still a central concept that the Afghan people have a strong desire for a future that is free from violence and meddling from outside sources. To forge a road towards a durable peace that tackles historical grievances and assures inclusive governance is the challenge that lies ahead.

Negotiating National Identity The history of resistance in Afghanistan has played a role in the formation of the country's national identity. In order to successfully negotiate this identity, it is necessary to reconcile the various religious, cultural, and ethnic components that are present. In order to cultivate a sense of togetherness and common purpose in the process of charting the

future course of the country, it is essential to strike a balance between these components.

Engagement with the international community and diplomacy: The engagement of the international community with Afghanistan continues to be a significant factor in determining the destiny of the country. When it comes to assisting Afghanistan in its transition toward stability, diplomatic efforts, foreign assistance, and cooperation are all quite important. With the lessons learned from historical disobedience, it is vital to take a collaborative strategy that respects the sovereignty of Afghanistan while also addressing problems on a regional and global scale.

Human Rights and Inclusivity: The lessons that have been learnt from Afghanistan's historical defiance highlight the significance of ensuring that human rights are protected and that inclusivity policies are implemented. When Afghanistan is navigating its future, it is of the utmost importance to protect the rights of all of its residents, regardless of their ethnicity, gender, or religious affiliation. This is necessary in order to construct a society that is just and equitable.

Reconstruction and Development of the Economy: The resiliency of Afghanistan's economy in the face of international interference and domestic wars has had a negative impact on the country's situation economically. The future of the nation is dependent on the successful completion of rehabilitation projects and initiatives for sustainable development. When it comes to fostering economic expansion and the development of infrastructure, the international community has the potential to play a crucial role.

As a result of Afghanistan's long-standing rejection against extremist ideas, it is imperative that they continue to place a strong emphasis on counterterrorism measures. Building a security infrastructure that is able to withstand attacks and addressing the underlying causes of extremism are both essential components in the process of securing long-term stability. For the purpose of averting the reappearance of terrorist threats, international coordination in these activities is of critical importance.

As a result of regional cooperation, the future of Afghanistan is closely connected to the dynamics of the area. For Afghanistan's stability to be maintained, it is essential to enhance regional economic integration, encourage collaboration among neighboring nations, and solve difficulties that cross international borders. In light of the historical disobedience that has occurred, a cooperative regional strategy has the potential to contribute to the maintenance of peace and security.

The persistent legacy that Afghanistan's historical defiance has left behind is one that continues to impact the nation's present and future. It is a monument to the unyielding character of the Afghan people that they have been able to persevere in the face of foreign occupation, internal disputes, and extreme beliefs. The complexity of Afghanistan's past are highlighted by the lessons that were learnt from moments of resistance, which also provide insights into how to formulate a strategy for moving forward.

As Afghanistan navigates its future, the international community plays a crucial role in providing support for the country's efforts to achieve security, peace, and development. When it comes to crafting a future that honors the sacrifices that have been made and nurtures a legacy of lasting peace and prosperity, acknowledgement of Afghanistan's historical defiance, comprehension of its complex character, and respect for the aspirations of its people are essential components. However, the resiliency that has been embedded in Afghanistan's past offers a beacon of hope for a brighter and more stable future. The difficulties are severe that Afghanistan must overcome.

9.1 Recapitulation of key points

In order to shed light on historical events, resistance movements, and global concerns, it is vital to distill the ideas gathered from diverse explorations as we engage on the journey of recapitulating crucial points while we are in the process of doing so. Lessons are carved onto the canvas of human experience, which is weaved through victories and sufferings. This canvas provides a canvas against which future horizons are envisioned, obstacles are tackled, and lessons are learned. With the purpose of providing a synthesized perspective on our collective journey, this recapitulation will traverse the enormous terrain of knowledge, weaving together threads ranging from historical disobedience to modern geopolitical complications.

A Recitation of Examples of Historical Disobedience:

Resilience Against Occupation: The annals of history are filled with instances of people who have shown themselves resilient in the face of occupation. The spirit of nations defending their sovereignty against external forces is a lesson that will never become obsolete. This can be seen in Afghanistan's unwavering fight to British colonization as well as in the relentless defiance that occurred throughout the Soviet-Afghan War. The persistent legacy of such disobedience serves as a guiding light for individuals who are navigating the present fights for self-determination.

Unity in the Face of difference: The lesson of unity in the face of difference is a recurring topic that may be found across multiple continents and generations. The broad ethnic and tribal makeup of Afghanistan, which serves as a microcosm of world variety, exposes instances in which differences were put aside in order to prioritize the achievement of a common objective. This oneness, which is shown most clearly in resistance movements, transforms into a powerful force that is capable of confronting formidable foes.

The impact of ideological conflicts Ideological conflicts have had a significant role in determining the manner in which history has unfolded. From the struggle against Soviet communism to the challenge of the Taliban's inflexible interpretation of Islam, the battles of ideas continue to echo throughout the course of history. When it comes to resolving conflicts and cultivating settings that respect different points of view, having a complete and nuanced understanding of the dynamics of ideologies becomes absolutely necessary.

Humanitarian Consequences of Conflict: Historical disobedience frequently exacts a toll in the shape of humanitarian catastrophes whenever it occurs.

As a harsh reminder of the costs of prolonged conflict, the repercussions of displacement, loss of life, and economic hardship, which resound through generations, are a constant reminder. The requirement to prioritize the well-being of civilians, give humanitarian help, and enable reconstruction activities stands out as a lesson for societies that are struggling to come to terms with the consequences of historical events.

Detailed Representation of the Geopolitical Complexities of the Present Day:

Viewpoints on Occupation Around the World The modern environment is characterized by continuous resistance movements and shifting viewpoints on occupation around the world. The accounts illustrate the complexities of power dynamics, international law, and the humanitarian effects of occupation. These narratives range from the battle for self-determination in Palestine to the pro-democracy movement in Hong Kong. Through the cultivation of conversation and the formulation of just resolutions, it is vital to have an understanding of the various world perspectives.

Concerning the role that civil society and global activism play in influencing current geopolitics, it is important to note that both of these phenomena are emerging as dynamic forces. It is through movements that advocate for human rights, fairness, and self-determination that the voices of communities who are marginalized are amplified. One of the defining characteristics of the contemporary era is the emphasis placed on the interconnectivity of global struggles, which is exemplified by the role that informed and involved citizens play in keeping governments and institutions accountable.

Warfare of Information and the Influence of the Media In this age where information is the dominant force, the battlefield extends to the many platforms of the media. There is a correlation between the influence of information warfare and media narratives on public opinion and the way in which conflicts are seen. In order to successfully navigate the intricacies of contemporary geopolitical environments, it is essential to acknowledge the significance of independent journalism and to cultivate critical media literacy.

Interactions between regional dynamics and global participation are what define the intricacies of the modern world. Regional cooperation and global engagement are two examples of these interactions. In the case of Afghanistan, for example, the future is dependent on regional collaboration, while global concerns such as climate change and pandemics require concerted efforts. Diplomacy skills, a respect for different points of view, and a dedication to the concept of shared global responsibility are all necessary components for successfully navigating through these complications.

A Reverberation of the Experiences Obtained and Prospects for the Future:

Capacity for Adaptation and invention: The lessons that can be learned from history highlight the significance of both adaptability and invention. It is the societies that have been able to successfully manage ideological transitions, accept technical developments, and display resilience in the face of hardship that have been successful over the course of history. When it comes to confronting the difficulties of the modern day, the ability to innovate and adapt continues to be an essential component.

Cooperation on a Global Scale for the Benefit of the Collective:

With the lessons that have been learned from global crises such as pandemics and climate change, it is clear that global collaboration is absolutely necessary for the collective well-being of the world. The United Nations and other such organizations serve as reminders of the possibility for collaborative efforts to address problems that are shared by several parties. It is becoming increasingly important to cultivate a feeling of global citizenship in order to successfully navigate the inter-related issues that the 21st century presents.

The rapid pace of technological progress necessitates a careful balance between innovation
and ethical considerations. This balance must be maintained in order to ensure that all parties involved are treated fairly. The lessons that can be learned from the historical developments in technology recommend that unbridled chases of progress be avoided because they have the potential to violate privacy, security, and ethical norms. When it comes to tapping into the potential benefits of technology, responsible innovation and a dedication to ethical principles are of the utmost importance.

Governance that is inclusive for the purpose of achieving social stability The historical struggles for civil rights and social justice highlight the significance of inclusive governance. In order to attain social stability, societies that place a higher priority on equality, fairness, and inclusivity are more likely to succeed. In the present day, efforts are being made to reform government structures and policies in order to meet the requirements of all parts of society. These efforts are informed by the lessons acquired from previous movements.

The narrative that emerges as a result of recapitulating significant themes from historical defiance to present geopolitical challenges is one that speaks to the resiliency of the human spirit, the impact of varied perspectives, and the imperative of ethical concerns in the process of traversing complex environments. The lessons that have been gained from historical conflicts and the problems that have been faced in the modern day converge on a common idea, which is that our road forward demands a commitment to unity, inclusivity, and communal well-being.

At this point in time, when we are standing at the crossroads of past experiences and potential futures, the call to action is crystal plain. In order to find a way ahead in the face of global difficulties, whether they are geopolitical wars, environmental disasters, or technological upheavals, it is necessary to combine historical knowledge with innovative thinking that is focused on the future. Not only does the recapitulation serve as a reflection on the past, but it also serves as a compass that directs us into a future in which the lessons of resiliency, unity, and ethical considerations move us towards a world that is more just, equitable, and sustainable.

9.2 Final thoughts on Afghanistan's historical defiance and its implications for the future.

As we contemplate the turbulent history of Afghanistan, which has been distinguished by unyielding resistance against external forces, we realize that we are at a crucial crossroads where the lessons of the past collide with the problems of the present, thereby determining the path that the nation will take in the future. Afghanistan's historical resistance left an indelible stamp on the nation's identity, marking everything from the country's struggle against British colonialism to its confrontation with the Soviet invasion and its struggle to come to terms with the complicated aftermath of the intervention led by the United States. Within the scope of this investigation, concluding ideas on Afghanistan's historical defiance and the enormous consequences it has for the future are being discussed.

The history of Afghanistan is a tribute to the perseverance of its people, and it serves as a guiding force throughout the country's history. The essence of Afghanistan's historical resilience can be defined as the capacity to withstand pressures from the outside, to navigate through periods of conflict, and to emerge with a spirit that has not been shattered by occupation or ideological impositions. This resiliency, which is profoundly ingrained in the characteristics of the Afghan people, acts as a directing force for the destiny of the nation.

Lessons That Teach Us About Unity and variety The historical defiance of Afghanistan is a reflection of the complicated dance that takes place between unity and variety. Despite its complexity, the mixed ethnic and tribal tapestry has shown moments of togetherness when confronted with threats from the outside. The experiences that were gained highlight the significance of recognizing and enjoying diversity while simultaneously cultivating a shared sense of national identity. This is an essential foundation for a future that is cohesive and welcoming to all populations.

The Price Paid During Prolonged Hostilities The historical struggle against foreign interference, which began during the time of British colonial rule and continued until the Soviet-Afghan War and beyond, serves as a sobering reminder of the price that was paid during prolonged hostilities.

The urgent need for durable peace-building activities is highlighted by the economic difficulties, societal disruptions, and humanitarian effects that have resulted from the conflict. It is imperative that a commitment be made to reconstruction, development, and addressing the underlying causes of instability in order to repair the scars left by continuous fighting.

Perspectives from Around the World and Diplomatic Engagement: Afghanistan's long-standing defiance sets the country into the larger context of international geopolitics. The intricacy of international relations is highlighted by the various points of view about occupation and intervention. In order to successfully navigate the future, mastery of diplomacy, the cultivation of alliances, and constructive engagement with the international community are all necessary. By gaining knowledge from previous encounters, Afghanistan has the potential to establish itself as a significant participant in regional and international forums, making a contribution to conversations that place an emphasis on cooperation and stability.

The Struggle for Inclusive Governance: Throughout its history, Afghanistan has had a number of different administrative structures, beginning with the monarchy, continuing through the turbulent years of Taliban control, and culminating in the following attempts to build democratic governance. It is becoming increasingly clear that the pursuit of inclusive governance, in which the rights and ambitions of all citizens are respected, is a fundamental component for the future of the nation. For the purpose of fostering stability and ensuring that everyone is represented, it is vital to construct institutions that are reflective of the different fabric that makes up Afghan society.

It is necessary to use a nuanced strategy in order to combat extremism because of the difficulties that are created by extremism, which were seen during the tenure of the Taliban and subsequent periods of insurgency. It is very necessary, in order to achieve long-term peace, to address the fundamental reasons of extremism, whether they be economic, social, or ideological. The experiences of historical disobedience highlight the significance of combating radical beliefs while also cultivating conditions that encourage knowledge, tolerance, and pluralism.

The Importance of International Partnerships International partnerships have been crucial in the formation of Afghanistan's history, from the provision of external support during resistance movements to the engagements that have taken place in the years following the attacks of September 11, 2001. The destiny of the nation will continue to be interwoven with the dynamics of the global community. In order to successfully navigate the complexity of the international stage, it is essential to cultivate constructive alliances that value Afghanistan's sovereignty, economic development, and social improvement.

Affirmation of Human Rights and Social Justice The historical defiance of Afghanistan against oppressive regimes brings into sharp relief the significance of human rights and social justice. The tenacity of people who strive for a more fair society is demonstrated by the efforts for civil rights, particularly those that have been waged by women and communities that have been marginalized. As the nation moves forward, it is imperative that the pursuit of social justice, gender equality, and human rights continue to be at the forefront of its aspirations.

Rehabilitation of the Economy and Sustainable Development: The economic landscape of Afghanistan, which has been formed by decades of violence, requires a coordinated effort toward rehabilitation and sustainable development. The combination of good governance and anti-corruption measures, along with international aid and investment, has the potential to stimulate economic growth.

Building a resilient economy requires a number of critical components, including the adoption of sustainable practices, the responsible utilization of natural resources, and the encouragement of entrepreneurial endeavors.

Optimism in the Face of Obstacles Afghanistan's historical defiance leaves a legacy of optimism, despite the numerous obstacles that it faces. There is a basis for a more promising future in Afghanistan that consists of the spirit of resistance, the desire of self-determination, and the perseverance that is engrained in the Taliban identity. The lessons that may be gained from past disobedience can serve as a source of inspiration, pointing the path toward a more stable and prosperous tomorrow. This is especially important as the nation navigates through the intricacies of post-conflict reconstruction.

For the purpose of closing views on Afghanistan's historical defiance and its implications for the future, the tale converges on a key juncture where the resiliency of the Afghan people meets the challenges of a world that is fast changing. For the purpose of charting the road that lies ahead, the lessons that were learned from resisting occupation, embracing diversity, and facing extremism serve as a compass. The future of Afghanistan is contingent on the country's dedication to inclusive governance, human rights, and sustainable development, which will be supported by diplomatic engagements and international collaborations.

As Afghanistan stands at a crossroads in its history, the echoes of defiance against oppression continue to reverberate, bearing with them the hopes of a nation and the aspirations of its people. The journey forward requires concerted efforts, both domestically and globally, to establish a future in which the wounds of the past become stepping stones toward enduring peace, stability, and prosperity. This is a requirement for successfully navigating the path forward. Afghanistan is a nation that is committed to form its destiny with perseverance, solidarity, and a vision of a better tomorrow. In the face of adversities, Afghanistan's historical defiance continues to serve as a beacon, illuminating the path for a nation that is determined to make its destiny.